DRIVING THROUGH POTHOLES

Financial Strategy and Life Lessons
for those looking to master personal finance
and rediscover the American Dream

By

Jesse M. Benedick

~~~

COPYRIGHT

TABLE OF CONTENTS

To my family for your endless love and guidance
To my heroes for always providing inspiration

PROLOGUE

What does the American dream mean to you? To our forefathers, the American dream was to live free from the oppression of a monarchy. A life of land, wealth, and happiness was available for anyone willing to make the trip. Today the American dream is most likely defined by accomplishing a set of goals; to be college educated, get married, start a family, and own a home. In today's financial map, the American dream still exists and you can still go there. It is available to anybody regardless of demographic. However, while the American dream still exists as a destination, the journey to get there has changed. The trip that used to be accomplished with ease is now a treacherous journey through the valley of debt. Many never make it out.

While the cost of the American dream has exponentially risen, the dream itself has turned into a nightmare for many. Societal pressure to keep up appearances is causing many to overextend financially and accumulate one debt after another. We're also less able to rely on our core immediate and extended family units, as our jobs are taking us further and further away. Displaced family units have become the new standard, further straining our finances. Due to these pressures, the personal finance vehicles of many went off the road so long ago, that the majority of those who accomplish the American dream today have driven through so many potholes that the Promised Land is now full of clunkers.

Don't be fooled into assuming our government will protect you; capitalism doesn't work that way. Capitalism is a for-profit political system. Capitalism is the foundation upon which our government house was built. In my opinion, the success of capitalism stems from the numerous "rags-to-riches" stories of immigrants, who came to this country with nothing, started a business, and hit the big time. Unfortunately, just as the Chinese have Yin and Yang (opposite complementary forces) there is also an equal negative side effect of capitalism. Due to capitalism, we now have a population of employees entrenched in debt. The middle class is being torn apart and, as they say, "the rich are getting richer, while the poor get poorer."

Capitalism is so entrenched in our government that it is quite common for the same attorneys who work for the largest corporations to later become politicians and run for office (with the big business' blessing). Big business buys campaigns and secures elections. These pandering politicians shape our legislation to be as advantageous as possible to the interests that keep them in office. When the same politicians eventually retire, or lose an election, the next natural step is to become a lobbyist and pander to the big business interests on the back end. Don't kid yourself into thinking capitalism doesn't depend on our population living a life of consumer debt. It is against the interests of capitalism (big business + our government) for you to have a financial education.

The cascading repercussions of the selling of capitalism masquerading as the American dream are unfortunately all around us. Think of the great recession of 2008. Against the best interests of our population, our own government (for the profits of big business) promoted the idea that everyone was entitled to a home, whether they could actually afford one or not. Our government marketed this unsound policy to our banking institutions, which swallowed the bait whole and backed one bad mortgage after another. As more people could suddenly afford mortgages, home values went through the roof. Prices shot to the moon, as financing (or overextending oneself) became the law of the land. The demand for housing created a building boom, due to the sudden lack of inventory. Therefore, the builders built so much that they created excess inventory. With high demand came high prices, and the government and our banks wrote even worse mortgages (Adjustable Rate Mortgages or ARMs with non-fixed rates) just to keep up. Never one to miss out on profits, Wall Street also got onboard the Titanic and rolled those same bad mortgages into complex derivatives (an investment vehicle, which nobody understood then or now). Wall Street then sold the snake oil (or complex derivative) to the highest bidder, for the greatest profit. This was capitalism on steroids. Completely unsustainable, and 100% predictable, the bad mortgages began failing one by one, going into foreclosure due to the increasing interest rates and lack of income to pay for them. One clunker after another broke down in the middle of the financial highway. When gridlock finally occurred, the entire system nearly crashed. The crumbling financial institutions that survived were ironically saved by our government, in the form of government bailouts in the trillions. Who truly paid for applying defibrillators to capitalism, though? You and I, the average taxpayers, were taken advantage of, and it was possible because we lacked the financial education to resist.

What about other aspects of the American dream? What about getting married? The pressure is on you to have a big wedding so all of your family and friends can attend. If you get married at the courthouse, the rest of your family will be somehow disappointed, since they missed an opportunity to get together and party on your dime. The social implications of getting married are just not what they used to be. Today, the expectation is to have an over the big top circus show of a wedding that comes at a price tag of anywhere from $25,000 to $100,000. Money well spent, right? Who is actually going to pay for this wedding anyhow?

What about that high paying job that you're entitled to? What do you mean it doesn't exist? This part will be a rude awakening to a lot of college graduates. If you didn't have an internship or don't already know somebody working for a particular employer or family business, good luck on that employment. You do not have a track record of measurable results, which is the only thing that matters when a bottom line is involved.

Starting a family while financing the rest of the American dream is going to set you up for years of stress generated by financial arguments. Outside of infidelity, the main reason couples split up is due to finances. Turn up the heat on the financial pressure cooker with new expenses that come from having a baby or babies and the stress of caring for a new child day and night. After a full one hundred and eighty degree life change, the family life you dreamed of may not be the life you've got.

What about "stuff"? Furniture, appliances, cars, clothes, electronics, sporting equipment, etc., are great things to buy new. They come new in a packaged box with wrapping. They have a nice shiny appearance and fresh smell. There is a crisp set of new instructions, but you don't need them because you're above instructions. They also make you feel good – for a few days anyhow. What happens, though, when the aura wears off and time goes by? Eventually, all of the things, which you thought you would never have to buy again, suddenly need to be replaced. You try to sell them, but either can't, or end up giving them away, due to the plummeted value.

I had a leather jacket, which I bought new for $450. It smelled great and was extremely soft. It was a designer jacket and "high-end." I loved the feeling of buying it. It also never fit quite right, as the arms were just slightly too long and covered my hands a little. Over time I realized when using it in cold weather that the leather got extremely cold, and actually made me colder. I naturally moved on to a wool pea coat. Attempting to sell the leather jacket, I listed it online, but received no inquiries. I eventually took it into the consignment shop. When we showed up to see how much money we made on the resale, my wife was handed $15. They sold it after two weeks for $35. My high quality, name-brand leather jacket had depreciated 97% in just a few years. I learned a great lesson that day about depreciation and depreciating assets.

According to Wikipedia, "The **sunstone** (Icelandic: *sólarsteinn*) is a type of mineral attested in several 13th–14th century written sources in Iceland, one of which describes its use to locate the sun in a completely overcast sky. A theory exists that the sunstone had polarizing attributes and was used as a navigation instrument by seafarers in the Viking Age." [1] My mission in this book is to serve you much like the sunstone, to be your guide on the road to financial freedom. I have made it my goal to ensure your navigational success—by providing a map. We will explore all of the facets of personal finance, including how to avoid potholes, what the framework of wealth looks like, debt management, all about investing, and how to make taxes work for you rather than against you. In this new reality we are going to strive for one singular goal: accomplish the American dream in a mint condition sports car rather than a rusty, creaky, hobbling, clunker. The American dream can and will be yours. Let me show you how.

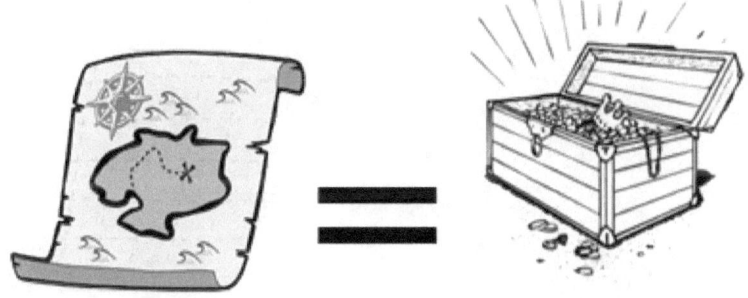

INTRODUCTION

Do you ever feel like you're not in control of your money? If at some point in the past you should made a different choice? Do you feel that if you had only known the ramifications of adding your signature to an ill-informed leap or loan, that at the time was really easy to sign up for, your future may have worked out differently? Do you wish you had only known about and taken a class on personal finance, budgeting, investing, or taxes? Maybe you felt or currently feel social or family pressure to deliver or keep up? Or maybe you're just getting started and your knowledge of personal finance is that of a beginner? Well, I've been or felt all of those too.

The purpose of this book is to be your financial map or sunstone. This book is intended to help you by exposing financial potholes, building a financial strategy, and executing a personal finance plan. We will remove finance-related stress, arguments, and challenges, while providing detailed experience, knowledge, and the financial tools and solutions for success. You will learn how to take control of your finances and become responsible and accountable for your future.

I am writing this book today as a guiding light for your financial journey. Join me on the road to financial freedom. Let's navigate the way ahead together. One cannot build a house without a foundation. Awareness, organization, and knowledge will lead to clarity.

The Interest Epiphany

My family and I began our journey to financial freedom one day while I was analyzing our yearly tax statement. We had paid $9,500+ in interest on our home mortgage. The numbers were shocking and I couldn't help but feel taken advantage of, gutted, ripped off, and entirely ignorant. Judging the loan on its own merit we had justified the interest payments as the cost of doing business. What we didn't realize was the collective interest. It was like we were punching the throttle in our speedboat, only to have one massive anchor of endless weight and length holding us in place, planted firmly in the bedrock.

I stepped outside to clear my head. I gave it a few minutes and stepped back inside. A few minutes later, I stepped back outside. Sitting down in my Adirondeck chair, I started to think about the people I knew who genuinely had money. I thought about their tax statements and how they made purchases. I thought about our bills in comparison to theirs. Then it happened.

A life-changing, long overdue realization or epiphany: the wealthy don't pay interest.

The more I thought about it, the more the statement hit home. We had been getting doubled-charged throughout our entire lives by living on loans and credit. This is how we were brought up, and this is what we knew. It was always easy to borrow money to pay for a new car or secure a college loan in hopes of a better job. We put incidental expenses, rent, and even our wedding on credit cards. We financed numerous vehicles that we really wanted or thought we needed. With each justification, it was like adding another shovel into the ground, making the hole we were in even deeper.

When we analyzed our house payments the money that was allocated for interest, escrow, and private mortgage insurance (PMI) dwarfed what was allocated for our principal balance. Out of our entire payment amount of $1,500, around $200 (or 13% of the payment) went to the principal balance. 87% of our payment held no benefit to us whatsoever. It was official: our speedboat was never going to pull anchor and it was only a matter of time before the motor burned out and the boat sank.

How could we be so naïve? I went straight to my loan documents and within the fine print of our loaned amount of $170,000, we had actually signed up to pay more than double that amount or nearly $350,000. I thought we were paying for a 1,418 square foot home, when in reality we were paying for double the house, or 2,836 square feet!

We began to investigate all of our household finances, including all of the loans and credit card debt held by my wife and me. With each debt, we discovered more of the same. When I finally compiled it all (including credit cards, car and student loans), we were paying over $12,000 per year in interest alone. So not only did we have one large anchor hanging off the speedboat, but eight other anchors of varying weight and length. We decided it was time to turn the motor off, let our circumstances soak in, and regroup. We had literally bottomed out.

Disappointed in ourselves, we began to reach out to friends and family for advice. What we didn't expect through was that the more people we talked to, the more we realized they were all in similar boats with their anchors also buried in the sand. Age, race, sex, and any other demographic didn't matter. We collectively were a society of people living paycheck to paycheck, burning out our motors trying to move our boats.

After quickly learning that our normal support systems were not going to be able to assist us with the guidance that we were looking for, we agreed that it was time to start searching for alternative solutions. What happened next was the beginning of our journey to the land of personal finance freedom.

Within each coming chapter I will include a section titled: *Our story...* that segment will cover a financial pothole based on real experience. Each segment will also follow the S.T.A.R.T. model, or Situation, Task, Action, Result and Takeaway. For an additional tip, the same model works very well for answering questions in a job interview...

Our Story – The Home Loan Pothole

• **Situation** – In late 2011, I discovered we were paying out well over $12,000 per year in interest on various debts consisting of our home loan, student loans, and credit card debts. Our Federal Housing Authority (FHA) first time home loan was costing $9,500+ a year in interest. In addition, because we decided to purchase our first home in 2008, we qualified for the first year of the new homebuyer program. The program was offering a $7,500 credit, which was instituted to promote home buying, and would therefore begin to prop up the housing market. The terms of the "credit" (it was actually an interest-free loan) were that following our first year, we would have to start repaying the credit to the tune of $500 a year for following 15 years immediately. Inexperienced and naïve, we justified the credit, because it was easy to justify another loan when we were not actively paying it back. Those were the terms and we accepted them. What we did not expect was that the following year, congress created new legislation to offer even more incentive money (up to $8,000). Additionally, within the new terms, the credit was no longer required to be paid back for those first time buyers in 2009 or any of the years of the program that followed. After researching and finding numerous other homeowners like us who were upset and taken advantage of in 2008, we decided that in addition to excessive interest we were paying, the 2008 homebuyer credit was the straw that broke the camel's back.

• **Task** – After a lengthy discussion and much consideration, my wife and I decided it was time to sell the home that we loved.

• **Action** – We placed our home up for sale for $189,000 in March of 2013. After nearly 50 showings, an open house, various ads, and lots of haggling with realtors, we finally sold the home six months later at an agreed upon sales price of $162,500. We were forced to move out into a dingy apartment.

• **Result** – Purposefully, we sold our home at a loss, which was a tough pill to swallow. Originally we purchased the home for $180,000. However, when we finally sold, our final sale price was $162,500. By selling the home for less than our original purchase price in 2008, with a difference that exceeded our home-buyer credit balance, we not only unloaded our terrible first-time FHA home loan, but we also erased our first time homebuyer credit debt.

•   **Takeaway** (or lesson learned) – I easily invested somewhere around $20,000 in improvements over the course of the five years that we owned our first home. Add to that $20,000, the fact that we sold our home for $17,500 less than what we purchased it at, and altogether we lost $37,500. Not figured in that calculation however, is the additional cost we were incurring in interest charges per year that added up to somewhere between $40,000 and $50,000 for those five years. Averaged out our net loss was in the ballpark of $80,000.

The situation above exposes only a few of the various potholes you can drive into while buying your first home. We feel that we were taken advantage of by the FHA loan process, as well as by naively believing in our government to create a fair and consistent program to promote home ownership. At the time it was originally created, the expectation of the homebuyer credit was that it had to be paid back. Nobody knew however, that starting in 2009, the legislation would completely change, but only for the new loans going forward. We were at a huge disadvantage to all of our peers who bought in 2009 and 2010, who built instant equity. We were on the other side of the coin, $7,500 in the hole.

One could argue that we drove straight into the home loan pothole, then immediately plowed into the homebuyer credit pothole. I would completely agree. Immediately following the interest epiphany we began our own research. The result of that research led to the next topic: The Framework for Wealth.

THE FRAMEWORK FOR WEALTH

What is wealth? I prefer the definition from Dictionary.com, which defines wealth as: "a great quantity or store of money, valuable possessions, property, or other riches; an abundance or profusion of anything; plentiful amount; the state of being rich" [2].

Financial Strategy for approaching The Wealth Framework

The first step to acquiring wealth is to study the traits of wealthy people. Most of us have a wealthy friend, neighbor, or relative who seems to defy the odds and always comes out ahead. We may also have an entrepreneurial, investment, or Wall Street hero who just continues to make deal after deal. They seem to live in a fantasy life without consequences, which we all envy. The question though, is how do they do it? If you start to study successful wealthy people in depth, specific themes and trends begin to emerge that collectively set them up for one success after another. By following a framework of guiding principles, they are able to acquire wealth by always being two steps ahead, much like thinking two to three moves ahead in a chess game. They are able to separate themselves by staying within the framework.

The wealthy were prepared as kids for success

Your chances for success in your personal finances either increase or decrease dramatically based on how well your family has prepared you to drive your own personal finance vehicle. Granted, everyone makes mistakes from time to time, but it is in your best interest to learn from your support system. Does your family follow the framework for wealth, or are they conditioned to habits of debt?

For many in the middle or lower class it can be very challenging to relearn how to manage finances. If you grew up in a home where the example set by your role models was that they always carried a mortgage, car loan or lease, credit card debt, student loan debt, financed payment plan(s), and any other type of recurring debt, you are going to find the wealthy path to personal finance to be very challenging simply because that is not what you know or what you grew up with. Many families often don't even realize that there is a problem; they go on buying fancy new cars, expensive electronics, and other depreciating assets. It isn't until years later that they realize they squandered their opportunities.

Those in the upper-middle to upper class grow up in a different environment. Many are used to seeing their role models make purchases in cash, and own property outright, whether it be autos, business, or real estate. They are taught to be conservative and live overhead free. Children in these families typically do not start out in debt either, nor do they add debt with credit cards or student loans. Rental properties for their first major purchase may serve as a source of passive income and the stage is set for life. Their parents are investors, who teach them to be investors first, and consumers second.

There is one major disclaimer with this section: do not think for one minute that those who appear to be doing the best always are. There are many people who are overextended, with a house, autos, country club memberships, etc., which they cannot afford. If you truly want to see something eye opening, look up foreclosed properties on a real estate website or app. It may truly surprise you, which houses are either the foreclosed or foreclosing that you never would have guessed. In those instances the property represents the illusion of wealth, rather than true wealth.

Family preparation is very important to getting an early start. If your family prepared you for a life of debt versus a life of wealth, don't blame them, because nobody taught them either. There will always be opportunities to learn and succeed. Take accountability, be your own person, and develop your own personal finance map.

The wealthy don't pay interest

The phrase above is directly indicative of how the wealthy approach personal finance; they do not take loans or run up credit card debts. The wealthy make their purchases in cash. By doing so they pay half price for housing, automobiles, education, businesses, and just about any other item, which they decide to acquire. It's easy to stay ahead of the game when you're paying half the price of everyone else.

The wealthy work for Unearned or Passive Income

Almost anyone who is wealthy counts on earning consistent passive income daily, weekly, or monthly. Defined by Wikipedia (2014, para. 1) as "an income received on a regular basis, with little effort required to maintain it."

Examples of passive income include the following:

- Earnings from a business that does not require the direct involvement from the owner or merchant

- Earnings from Internet advertisements on websites

- Interest from a bank account

- Ownership of natural resources. (Ownership of a property with wind turbines, highway billboards, oil, natural gas, etc.)

- Royalties from publishing a book, licensing a patent; a computer software product [3]

- Digital products such as music, jingles, eBooks, images, etc.

- Ownership of E-commerce websites that charge fees based upon transactions (eBay, Etsy, Paypal, Square, etc.)

- Lottery winnings

- Military retirement

• Peer-2-Peer Lending

• Pensions

• Personal businesses that rent space (Storage Unit facilities, Antique malls, Marinas, etc.)

• Residential or commercial real estate rental property income (apartment buildings, homes, shopping malls, etc.)

The Wealthy Make the Tax Code Work for Them.

It is often pointed out in the news media (especially during election season) that the wealthiest individuals as well as companies making the most money are paying the lowest percentage in taxes. Those making earned income (or less money) are routinely taxed at a higher rate, and therefore feel that the system is rigged. However, what is routinely missed in the discussion, is how exactly the wealthy do it. The answer to that question is actually pretty simple and not the big secret that you may think it is: the wealthy embrace the tax code by doing what the government gives incentives for.

• The wealthy invest in private business by starting, buying, improving, and maintaining businesses of various strengths, sizes, and niches. The tax code offers numerous incentives for business owners not because they are intended to make the rich richer, but rather to bolster the economy as a whole by providing jobs and taxable earned income on those jobs, back to the government.

• The wealthy earn a majority of their income as passive or unearned income, which overall is taxed at a far lower rate. Once again, in return for bolstering the economy as a whole by providing jobs and taxable earned income that feeds back to the government, the wealthy are provided incentives to make passive income investments.

• The wealthy invest in property and land that either provides housing or has the potential to provide housing.

In summary, by providing housing and jobs through investment, the wealthy are able to build up their passive or unearned income in combination with receiving tax break incentives. We will expand the topic of incentives in greater detail in a later chapter: The Tax Code.

The Wealthy Diversify

Whether it is a new business or investment opportunity, the wealthy always diversify, purposefully. To mitigate risk, the wealthy never place all of their eggs into one basket.

What separates wealthy entrepreneurs from novice investors is the ability to view each business opportunity objectively versus subjectively. Novice entrepreneurs will endlessly chase an idea due to their own subjective attachment, much like a dog chasing its tail. The wealthy investor on the other hand, is chasing his tail, while playing with a ball and chew toy at the same time.

Wealthy entrepreneurs often become very successful by consistently following the same formula: they invest, re-invest, profit, and move on. The wealthy listen to the market and always let it dictate their next move, most importantly because the market always changes. It is often the case that it is much more difficult to keep the same business with the same business model going, versus starting a new business with a new model. By diversifying, the wealthy enter new markets, learn new skills, and often become even more successful.

Two examples of public figures that share a visible track record of diversification are Elon Musk and Richard Branson. In the case of Musk, he was one of the original cofounders of x.com (which later merged with Confinity), who "operated a subsidiary called PayPal." After abandoning the idea to co-brand PayPal with x.com, Musk removed the x.com brand, and refocused his efforts on a "viral growth campaign" for Paypal. In October 2002, PayPal was acquired by eBay for US$1.5 billion. Post PayPal, Musk founded Tesla Motors (the California electric car maker) and SpaceX, which were "awarded a $1.6 billion NASA contract on December 23, 2008, for 12 flights of its Falcon 9 rocket and Dragon spacecraft to the International Space Station."[4] In a similar case, Branson, started "his first business venture at the age of sixteen; a magazine called *Student*. In 1970, he set up a mail-order record business," and "in 1972, he opened a chain of record stores, Virgin Records, later known as Virgin Megastores." Today, "he is best known as the founder of Virgin Group, which comprises more than 400 companies." [5] Branson's latest business opportunity is in Virgin Galactic, which hopes to commercialize space travel at a premium. So how is it that one entrepreneur who started a website, and another who started a student magazine are now invested in space travel? Both Musk and Branson follow the market above all else, and therefore their resumes document diversification. They each have transitioned into new opportunities numerous times based upon what the market has told them, which is exactly what you need to do: start businesses.

The Wealthy Capitalize on Natural Talent

Everyone has something they do better than someone else; however, not everyone pursues what they are best at. The wealthy capitalize on their natural skills, by doing what they love to do. They literally follow their passion as far as it will take them. They love what they do, rather than dread what they do, and because of that simple fact they are often more successful. The wealthy are not looking for the pot of gold, but rather for the rainbow. The pot of gold is just a bonus.

A great example of taking a skill and running with it is the "Oracle of Omaha," Warren Buffett, who I consider to be the greatest investor of all time. With a steady value investment strategy and a frugality that keeps him grounded, Buffet has amassed great wealth. Believe it or not, Buffet still lives in the same house in Omaha, Nebraska, that he purchased for $31,500, in 1957. Clearly the money isn't why Buffett is in the game, but rather because his true passion is value investing. It is not, and was never about the money. Proof is in the fact that he has "pledged to give away 99 percent of his fortune to philanthropic causes." [6]

The wealthy surround themselves with the best team

The wealthy surround themselves with experts because having the best team can sometimes make the difference between success and failure. The wealthy inherently know that they do not have all of the answers, and therefore they must be resourceful in finding, relying, and keeping the best experts on their team to assist in accomplishing their goals. Some examples of experts that you might find on team wealthy may include, but not be limited to, the following:

- Accountants, Bankers, Attorneys
- General Contractors and Subcontractors
- Experienced Consultants
- Personal Assistant, Secretary or Right-Hand Man
- Young, innovative talent

The Wealthy Implement A Risk Structure

A hallmark trait of those who are wealthy is that they always have resale value in mind regarding any financial purchases or transactions. Projecting resale value can immediately expose whether a possible business deal is of high or low financial risk. With research and assessment, the wealthy ensure that they only pursue low-risk financial deals, which guarantee to leave their finances in the black. If the deal has red flags, they always walk, because there is always another deal.

Examples of items the wealthy may purchase with resale in mind are:

> • Autos - The wealthy buy in cash, at auction, and often write off vehicles for business-related purposes.

> • Businesses - A Venture Capitalist will invest in a struggling business with the plan to quickly downsize, rehab, reshape, and make it once again profitable, specifically for resale.

> • Commercial and Residential Real Estate - The wealthy pay for most real estate in cash and therefore pay consistently lower purchase prices in addition to zero interest.

• Land - Developers often buy land at the lowest cost possible only to upsell to builders, who then upsell to potential homeowners, with one flip following another.

The Wealthy Buy With Cash

By making the vast majority of their purchases with cash, the wealthy receive discounted pricing on all of their purchases. They also have more opportunities fall into their lap simply because they pay in cash. A quote to live by is that "A seller's favorite buyer is one who pays in cash," which I firmly believe. Whether it is flipping autos, businesses, commercial and residential real estate, or land, cash transactions rise to the top of the competition every time.

The Wealthy Prepare for and Manage Life Events

Common life events have the ability to easily derail your life plans and financial goals, which is why the wealthy plan for them. Whether it is an inherent trait, or a learned skill of risk assessment, the wealthy have their affairs in order, in preparation for significant life events. Typical mitigation strategies include: insurance (auto, homeowners, life, etc.), emergency funds and/or savings, available access to expert advice, or even by continuously adding streams of passive income. As opposed to the average person, the wealthy are usually more prepared to weather the storm of a significant life event.

Some examples of significant life events include:

- Birth of a child
- Catastrophic Event (Act of God) – Hurricane, Earthquake, Tornado, etc.
- Family Planning
- Home Purchase or Loss
- Job Loss
- Lawsuits
- Marriage (to include weddings) or Divorce
- Sickness or Death of a family member

It should be pointed out that often it only takes the fallout of one life event to start unraveling another. Before you know it, you could find yourself without health, wealth, and security. For example, if you get sick or have a car accident without insurance, you could easily find yourself on the hook for tens of thousands of dollars. Due to the same illness, you could eventually lose your job, strain a marriage into divorce, lose your home, and before you know it, bankruptcy will be your only option. Years of your life could be consumed with repaying the debt or dealing with the bankruptcy fallout, all from one significant life event. The bottom line is that preparation is the key to managing life events and the wealthy are often prepared. Plan for the worst and hope for the best.

The Wealthy Execute

One of the biggest differences between those who are wealthy and those who are not is that the wealthy execute. They not only come up with great ideas, but they actually follow those ideas through to conclusion. How often have you thought of a really great idea, only to talk yourself out of it because it sounded like too much work? Or you had a really great idea but didn't know where to start, so rather than map out a research plan you simply decided to give up? The reality is that this simple concept is actually quite challenging for many of us. A lot of people find themselves hung up in the details, and either don't want to, or don't know how to take that critical next step. Seeing an idea through from start to finish creates a strong sense of accomplishment and a foundation of confidence. For those who take the first step, let alone the many steps that it will take to follow an idea through from start to finish, the payoff can be extremely rewarding.

The Wealthy Fail, But Never Give Up

If you bet against successful people you are going to lose. Often it is the most successful ones who prove they can achieve their goals again and again against great odds because they never give up. It is the drive of successful people that leads to wealth. This is why many entrepreneurs who firmly believe in themselves can push their product and influence into eventual success. They often do what the critics say cannot be done, but what the market says should be done. Many of my financial heroes are entrepreneurs with this specific skillset.

- Richard Branson (founder of Virgin)
- Elon Musk (founder of Paypal, Tesla Motors, SpaceX)
- Jeff Bezos (founder of Amazon.com)
- Jack Dorsey (founder of Square, Twitter)
- Marc Cuban (founder of Broadcast.com, owner of the Dallas Mavericks, TV personality)

When the wealthy fail, they don't give up. The wealthy take calculated risks, fail often, and eventually succeed. It is often said that: "failure is the fire that forges the steel for success." I believe this to be true.

Our Story – The Family Planning Pothole

• **Situation** – In 2008, we were blessed with the birth of our son Vin. The little guy changed our lives completely. At that point in my life, I was twenty-six years old. My job required that I travel nearly 75% of the time, and because of that, I was compensated with a substantial amount of salary, overtime, per diem, and big time benefits, such as a company car. Each time I was home, though, we became more and more attached. We really gelled as a family, which made it harder and harder each time I received the phone call to leave. At first Vin didn't really know who I was, so it was hard on me, yet easy on him. As he started to become attached to me, I became attached to him. He would break down crying when he and my wife would drop me off at the airport. I wanted to punch myself in the face. It was an unbearable experience.

• **Task** – I knew it was time to make a change. I needed to get off the road and go into the office, so that I could be a real father to my son.

• **Action** – After being on the road for five years and nine months I applied, interviewed, and transferred into a local office near our home.

• **Result** – When I got off the road we instantly had our family back together, which was awesome. It was also great knowing that I was no longer going to be called out to another state on short notice. We could plan for family events and really build a life together. Of course, with every action there is an equal or opposite reaction: the financial transition. I had been making a base salary, differential, overtime, and per diem while in the field. I also had a company car with free gas, free maintenance, and all of the other perks that come with being on the road, like platinum status on hotels and airlines. I lost everything but my base salary. In an instant I lost somewhere in the ballpark of $30,000 a year. It was a rough transition. Instantly we went from being able to do what we wanted whenever we wanted to do it, to being badly overextended. Our finances were a mess. We had to make cuts wherever we could just to break even. We couldn't even afford groceries. Suddenly we realized that debt and bills were suffocating us. We were spending over 95% of my take home salary on bills. It was a brutal, painful existence, and again, something had to give for us to survive. We were forced to evolve.

• **Takeaway** – The pay cut was brutal, but it was necessary to open our eyes to how far we were overextended. Steadily, one-by-one, we began to pay off our smaller debts and remove each bill, one-by-one. At this time I also began applying for new jobs. When I was on the road it was impossible to attempt to interview while being states away. Now that I was home it was time to take advantage of it. After three months of working in the local office, and six years total for the company, I applied, interviewed, and was offered a higher position with a similar company, which paid nearly $11,000 more. It was a no-brainer decision and thus we turned the page on a difficult chapter in our lives.

Conclusion

Are you feeling inspired to become wealthy? I hope so. You definitely aren't reading this to go broke. The point of this chapter was to delve in detail into the traits of those who are wealthy. If you are now beginning to spot areas of opportunity within your own personal finances, your own framework for wealth is forming. Always remember that in times of doubt regarding wealth and financial strategy that you need to ask yourself what the wealthy would do if faced with your same circumstance. Would the wealthy take that high interest loan or apply for that high interest credit card, just to make that purchase you don't really have to make? The wealthy wouldn't be paying interest, I can tell you that much. Then again, I already have, and you already know this.

Money Tips

• What is your definition of wealth? Write down your goals, financial and otherwise. Where do you see yourself in the future? What do you want to accomplish?

• Take out a piece of paper and tape it to the wall. Write the phrase "the wealthy don't pay interest." Look at that piece of paper on a daily basis.

• Consider the *"Our story"* segment. What might you have done differently if this happened or could happen to you?

• If you are planning to purchase your first home in the near future, analyze loan terms, where the money is coming from and the interests involved.

• What skill can you capitalize on?

AWARENESS

The first step toward improvement is to become mindful of what you do not know. Financial ignorance can and will cost you. Think of all of the athletes and entertainers who have squandered everything and lost millions in bad business deals, cars, clothes, friendships, handouts, investments, jewelry, marriages, mansions, partnerships, consultants, managers, and any other exorbitant, wasteful purchases. Think of all of the rich people who lost money in Ponzi schemes, by blindly trusting a criminal masquerading as a financial expert. Half of the group completely mismanaged their money themselves, while the other half turned it over to someone else to mismanage for them (or skim money off the top). Talk about driving through potholes.

Typically those who are not aware also tend to live at, above, or well beyond their means. With each rung they climb up the ladder, the financially ignorant tend to invest in liabilities (bigger house, fancier cars, expensive clothes, high price dinners, gambling, etc.) rather than investing into streams of unearned or passive income. All it takes is one slip-up or unexpected life event to put that car into a pothole it won't be coming out of.

After the car is fully disabled in the pothole for good (usually after years of financial ignorance), a common regret of those who were financially ignorant, is that they wish someone had taught them how to manage their finances themselves. I'm here to tell you that, typically, you do not become aware unless either your family raises you to be aware, or until you've hit the final pothole to disable your vehicle. Consider yourself lucky to be aware.

The Almighty Credit Score

The system is built so that you cannot get loans without credit. Showing that you are a low risk because you repay your loans is what you are sold and told to do. If you are a high risk due to past repayment issues, you're going to be charged a higher rate. The catch here is, why are you loaning money that you don't have anyway? Stop borrowing money, stop overextending yourself, and learn to fully understand credit scores.

Many of the most prominent financial experts say to dump the credit score altogether and pay in cash, but by bucking the system they are somewhat recommending you play with a double-edged sword. I agree that you should make as many of your purchases as possible in cash only, and more importantly, if you do not have the cash, you should not be securing any loans. On the other hand, though, if you have no credit, you may (or may not) run into adverse consequences, which you should be aware of. Job applications within the financial industry typically require a full credit check. If you have no credit, you have no score, and you ultimately will have no job, because you won't even be able to secure an interview. In the case of starting up utilities on your place of residence, most utility companies will require a credit check, or you may incur excessive start-up fees (which can be nearly triple the cost of a normal start-up fee for someone with a decent credit score). If you are renting an apartment or home, the landlord will almost always perform a background check that includes a check of your credit. No credit = no rental, unless you're paying the entire term of the lease up front.

I personally recommend being mindful of your credit score and its potential application to your personal situation. In other words, much like an emergency credit card, you never know when you may need it. Consider your credit score a dirt road on the journey to financial freedom; even though the road is available for travel, you are typically not going to use it, as there are much better ways to get where you are trying to go.

Don't Take the Marketing Bait

At home, during school, on the TV, Internet, radio, and in social media, we are bombarded daily with marketing advertisements and incentives to delay our arrival in the land of financial freedom, and instead get off on the nearest exit. Much like fishermen dangling a baited fishhook, the advertisers hope you're a curious little fish who will decide to come in for a little nibble. Talk about foreboding finance. Don't take the bait. Be patient, and let the guy next to you take the bait. Wait and see what happens. Much like the theme of this book, learn from others' mistakes, and let the other guy hit the tractor-trailer tire in the middle of the financial highway.

Financial Strategy for Awareness

Awareness starts when you begin to ask questions. Why is it that the credit card companies send me letters every day? Why do I constantly receive letters to refinance? Why are there so many pharmaceutical commercials during the evening news, and why do they turn up the volume extra loud? Why do furniture stores offer me payment plans with zero annual percentage rate (APR) financing? Why does our culture put pressure on us to drive a new car rather than a used one? The more questions you ask yourself about what is in it for you, the more you realize what's *not* in it for you. Financial interests (banks, governments, suppliers, manufacturers, dealers, etc.) are constantly offering incentives to blind you. Much like a neon billboard, stare long enough and you're going to plow straight into a pothole. Keep your eyes on the road. Financial strategy for awareness requires

41

that you ask questions, researching the "why," and developing your own knowledge of what is and what is not a pothole.

Financing/Leasing a Vehicle

Have you ever purchased or leased a brand new car? Bought something flashy that you could show off to your friends, family, and coworkers? The experience includes an awesome new car smell, stylish paint, and shiny wheels. Maybe it is a really fast sports car, or a pick-up truck with a lift kit? Deep down we all want to drive a new car or truck with all of the bells and whistles. The question though, is at what cost? Could you find something comparable used?

I personally dread going into car dealerships. I'm not sure if it's the sales people, endless haggling, or my own anxiety toward the feeling that I am about to be taken advantage of. Ultimately, I just feel uncomfortable. First off, I know that a new car or truck is a rapidly depreciating asset. Secondly, I know that in addition to the cost of the car or truck, the cost of insurance, maintenance, and fuel, will also add up significantly to the overall cost of ownership. I know that the dealership will try to pressure me into purchasing a protection plan, which I will never use, at the cost of raising my monthly payment even further. I also know that even when I park my brand new car or truck in the back of the lot, away from everyone just to avoid door dings, that somebody will ultimately end up parking right next to me, and obliviously open their car door straight into mine. No matter how hard I try, the vehicle will degrade and depreciate. It is important to keep in mind, that whether the vehicle is brand new, like new, gently used, or poorly used, all vehicles truly have one thing in common: you only need them to get you from point A to point B.

The average auto-loan term increased to 66 months during the first quarter. Making matters worse, nearly 25% of all new vehicle loans originated during the quarter had terms extending out 73 months to 84 months. The average amount financed for a new vehicle loan also reached an all time high of $27,612. Per Melinda Zabritski, Experian Automotive's senior director of automotive credit, "consumers are clearly stretching the loan term to lower monthly payments. The benefit of a longer-term loan is the lower monthly payment; however, the flip side of that is consumers can find themselves paying more in interest or being upside-down on their loan if they seek to trade their vehicle in early." Also noted in the same article, the average monthly payment for a new vehicle loan hit a record high of $474 in the first quarter.

(McWhinnie, "Are Americans Filling Up on too Much Debt?" 2014, para. 2-5). [7]

In other words, we are now not only paying more for vehicles that we cannot afford, but in order to justify the overextension, our society is shifting toward vehicle financing options that average between five and a half to seven years. Five and a half to seven years is an extremely long time to tie up your income in a depreciating asset.

Let's assess the options for vehicle ownership:

• Option 1 - Finance a vehicle (which you cannot afford) by extending the loan term to 84 months (seven years). By the time you've finally paid off the loan, you will have lost so much money in depreciating value that your monthly payment (or overpayment) will become a daily reminder of how poor your choice was. By the time you finally pay off the vehicle, you'll be so high in mileage that you'll already be well on your way to financing your next vehicle, continuing the cycle of perpetually paying for depreciating assets in the form of car payments. Verdict: pothole.

• Option 2 – Much like Option 1, Option 2 involves financing, but rather than making it to the end of the marathon (seven years), you decide you need a new vehicle due to personal, family or business reasons, and therefore choose to trade your vehicle in. You most likely will have negative equity due to the rate at which your new car has depreciated (your car lost half of its value the moment you drove it off the lot). The negative equity will be tacked onto your new deal and the cycle –

will actually get even worse: you will have no down payment or equity to place toward the next vehicle. Verdict: pothole.

• Option 3 – You decide to lease a new car. By doing so, you have guaranteed that at the end of three years, you will own nothing; need another car, and another down payment. You also may owe additional money to the dealer if you have gone over your yearly mileage quotas, which are typically 12,000 miles per year. Your credit score will look great, but other than the score, you won't have much to show for your money at the end of the lease term. Again, you have booked your ticket as a member of the rat race and will continue the cycle of perpetual payments. Verdict: pothole.

• Option 4 – You have decided to purchase a used car from a dealer. Whether financing the purchase of a used car from a dealer, or not you are still subject to dealership fees, as well as their cost of overhead (sales lot, sales people, electricity, etc.). Financing is never recommended; however, if you are making your purchase from a dealer with cash, you are still overpaying by potentially thousands. Verdict: pothole.

• Option 5 – You have decided to purchase a used car from a private seller. Financing, again, is never recommended. If you are making the purchase with cash, you will need to invest your money first into having the vehicle checked out beforehand by an experienced mechanic, as well as obtaining the CARFAX report on the vehicle. If the car and vehicle identification number (VIN) check out, make the purchase and look forward to not being saddled with car payments. Verdict: Not a pothole, and the best choice of all five options.

Vehicle financing is a major pothole on the road to financial freedom. Choose carefully, and avoid options 1-4 if you can. Sometimes, it may be advantageous to pursue one of options 1-4, if you are purchasing the vehicle strictly for a business. However, please be mindful that for most people purchasing a personal vehicle option 5 is the best path to avoid a pothole.

Home Financing

Paying for a house in cash is extremely challenging because it requires great discipline, sacrifice, a strong family, or a substantial amount of luck, i.e. inheritance. Set a goal, and try living rent-free or low-rent with your mom/dad/brother/sister, other relatives, etc. See how much money you can save when you're not paying rent. Also, try combining incomes with family/friends. Combining finances has the potential to get you ahead fast if you make a plan. Pair up with your family or best friend. I like to think of the many multi-generational immigrant families, where they all live under the same roof. By combining their incomes, they pay off their house debt significantly faster than you or I would on our own. The result is that many become small business owners, because they have collateral.

Choosing the combined-income plan to get ahead does; however, come with a price: sacrificing independence. You may have to sacrifice going away to a big university (out-of-state, as well as in-state). Your social life may also take a dive, if you continue to live under your parents' or siblings' roof, while your friends go away for school or the military. The plan will also likely delay the start of your adult life (kids, marriage), but in the end, may be a blessing in disguise. Would you rather start your adult life with financial security of a substantial down payment or a house that's paid for in full, or would you prefer to kick start your twenties, thirties, and beyond, overburdened, broke, and in a constant state financial strife? The answer is obvious.

I personally recommend shooting for a savings amount of 20% or more of the home loan, which you are applying for. If you put down less than 20% you are going to be saddled with PMI (private mortgage insurance) to the tune of $100 - $200 per payment. Unlike other types of insurance that you take out to cover yourself, the mortgage company is essentially taking out insurance against you (the risk). You know yourself, and whether or not you are a risk or not; however, the bank doesn't care. Ultimately, you are paying for nothing, with no benefit to yourself, and throwing away thousands of dollars to appease a policy and check a box in a computer program. In order to remove PMI, mortgage companies will stipulate that you first pay down the mortgage to the point of having a loan-to-value ratio of 80% or less. Some mortgage companies also require that you pay PMI for at least five years before they will even consider your request to remove it. In the post-housing crisis changes, effective June 3, 2013, if you take out an FHA loan with a loan-to-value ratio in excess of 90%, removing PMI is not an option (Green, D. 2013). [8]

If you're currently stuck paying PMI, you do have a few options available to you. In the case of paying for PMI on a loan, which is not FHA, pay the loan-to-value ratio down to the 80%, and request the mortgage company remove the PMI. If on the other hand, you have an FHA loan with PMI, it may be best to sell the property and invest a few years into renting, regrouping, or combining incomes. Pay off all of your debts and correct your future. Think of it as taking your car in for a 100,000-mile tune-up.

When choosing financing you will also need to weigh whether to apply for a 30 year or 15 year loan, and whether you would like your rate to be fixed or an adjustable rate (ARM). Your goal for terms should always be for the shortest amount of time possible, or the 15 year product. Regarding fixed versus adjustable rate, it really comes down to risk. For example, the low risk option is always going to be a fixed rate; however, with a fixed rate, it is fixed, and you are stuck with it until you sell or refinance. With an adjustable rate mortgage the rate of the loan could potentially skyrocket if the economy is doing well, or plummet if the economy is tanking. Prior to the most recent recession, ARMs were being sold left and right. Many of those who signed up for ARMs found themselves priced out of their homes, as the rates continued to skyrocket with corresponding home values. Eventually, when the bubble burst, those with ARMs, who were able to weather the storm, actually had their rates plummet to well below that of many who had fixed rates, thus they made quite a savings. If you have the money to afford a 15 year fixed product, the rate will be so low, that the savings you would have made with an ARM, most likely wouldn't be worth it. Shoot for the 15 year fixed rate with 20% down.

Always remember that it is easy to justify a loan when you are not actively paying it back.

If you plan to buy your first home with only 3–5% down, not only are you going to get saddled with PMI, but you are also going to be paying somewhere around $7,500 - $10,000 a year interest. Tack on a 30 year product with an adjustable rate and you may find yourself on a slippery slope. Is the independence worth it? Once again, the answer is obvious.

Government-backed Student Loans

There is currently more than one trillion dollars held in the United States in student loan debt. According to Kiplinger.com (2014):

> One trillion dollars could buy 41,999,160 new cars at between $20,000 - $25,000 each, 5.6 million homes, 140 billion hours of work at $7.25 an hour, pay for the salary of congress (both the House and Senate) at $174,000 each for the next 10,742 years, or even more eye-popping, in a Certificate of Deposit (CD) at just 1.29 %, the interest on one trillion dollars would equal 12.9 billion annually [9].

Need I say more? Maybe I should. According to the Ellis, B. (2013, para. 1), the average student graduates with a tab of $29,400 [10]. Is it becoming obvious why servicers as well as the federal government have quite an interest in student loan debt? Can you say "cha-ching?"

The irony within the student loan crisis is capitalism. For the same reasons that our capitalist society wants you to become college-educated, the same principles are actively hustling our students by promoting absurd debt through bad rules and unfair tax practices. The ballooning student loan debt bubble is becoming a larger drag on the economy each day. Unfortunately, the vast majority of our elected leaders (or rich attorneys, bankers, and CEOs), are so far removed from the average person, that they don't even see that we have a problem. The vast majority of our elected officials are so out of touch, that they honestly cannot relate, while the ones who do understand the problem, choose to ignore it, because the same interests who paid for their campaigns are wielding significant influence on the issue (against the will of the people).

College graduates are now carrying debt well into their thirties and beyond. Graduates are also being forced to delay life events such as marriage, children, and a home purchase, due to student loan debt. It should also be noted that, unlike other types of debt such as credit card debt, a government-backed student loan cannot be removed by filing for bankruptcy. If you fail to repay a government-backed student loan, the government has the option to not only garnish your wages, but it can even come after your social security! Talk about the pothole of all potholes.

A massive misconception also exists within the false hope known as "student loan forgiveness." The concept itself is misleading, as it implies that forgiveness is available to anyone, when in reality, it is only available for a very select few. $4,725 is available for volunteers of Americorps or Volunteers in Service to America (VISTA). A requirement exists of 12 months of service or 1,700 hours. Elementary or secondary school teachers that serve students who are disabled or from low-income families may qualify for forgiveness of 15% of their student loans for the first two years, 20% for the 3rd and 4th years and 30% for the 5th year. Non-profit legal and medical studies offer forgiveness for those practicing law "in the public interest or non-profit positions," students conducting clinical research, or veterinarians who commit to work in a shortage area for three years. Students actively engaged in military service within the Army National Guard can earn up to $10,000, while those that are actively deployed in "fulltime service" within the armed forces "in areas of hostilities or imminent danger," as well those working as law enforcement or corrections officers, may be eligible for cancellation of the loan [11]. In case you missed it, I would venture to say that student loan forgiveness probably applies to less than 5% of all government-backed student loans.

Levels of forgiveness also vary dramatically by the type of the loan (Stafford, Perkins, Consolidated, etc.) as well as the forgiveness program, and whether it is state of federal. Consider, that if the average student graduates with $29,400 in debt, that $4,725 (or even $10,000) is just 16% (or 34%) toward the loan. In reality the supposed, pie-in-the-sky, forgiveness amount, is nowhere near enough to pay off the loan, but rather a drop in a bucket with a hole in it. Unless you have chosen one of the select career paths or volunteer opportunities above, you can all but forget about loan forgiveness, which brings us to the next scam: deferment.

Often times a loan servicer or program may offer the student deferment based upon financial inability to repay the loan or active volunteer service. What deferment really means is that your payments are put on hold, while the accruing interest on the principal balance is not. So in other words, when you graduate from college and cannot find a job, there is no safety net. A good analogy would be if you have ever put your cable or cellular contract on hold for six months. At the end of the six months you would still owe for the time the contract was on hold; however, with deferment, interest on the principal balance has been building the entire time you had the contract on hold. What this means is that a student loan on deferment could easily balloon the principal balance anywhere from 25% to 50% greater, based on the amount of time it is in deferment. Someone with a loan amount of $15,000 at 6%+, who defers their loan for just a year or two, could easily wind up with a balance anywhere from $20,000 - $25,000. I know this last point for a fact, as it happened to us.

Ultimately, the worst part about student loan debt is that often times what was promised is not the end result. Either the student who took the loan never graduated, or when they did graduate, they were unable to line their new degree up with a job that pays enough to repay the loan. Avoid the pothole. The best strategy regarding federally backed student loans is to never apply for them in the first place. There are lots of other ways to pay for school that do not include borrowing money from our government, such as:

1. **Scholarships** – A good scholarship has the potential to pay for your entire undergraduate degree. In my experience, The Bright Future's Scholarship (offered in Florida), paid for 75% of my undergraduate degree, and I qualified for the scholarship by maintaining a B average. If I had maintained an A average, I could have qualified for the even more generous version of the Bright Future's Scholarship, which covered 100%. For information on scholarships available in your state, your high school administration counselors should be able to assist, while another avenue is to search online by typing in your state and the word "scholarship."

2. **Family money** is another way to pay for schooling. Whether it is a prepaid scholarship, a savings bond, or a Trust fund, there are various ways, which your family can contribute to your adult education. In my case, my father contributed to a Florida Prepaid Scholarship, which ended up covering all of my additional expenses outside of the 75% provided by the Bright Future's Scholarship. Your folks can also choose to let you live rent free, which can free you up to pay for it yourself.

3. **Employer-paid** (military included) – may be the most gratifying option to pay for your adult education. Many

54

employers will pay for you to get a Bachelor or even a Masters, if your chosen degree is within a field applicable to their business model. Typically an employer will require you to work for the company for a specified period of time before they will consider funding your education. Once you meet the time requirement; however, your employer's Human Resources Department as well as your manager will probably have to sign off on your request. When the request is approved, your employer will reimburse you based on the grades you obtain. Your employer also may have a stipulation that upon graduation, you stay with the company for a specified number of years. The catch with this option is that it is not easy, and will require significant dedication, in addition to quite a few late nights.

4. **Your last college option** (which I consider the nuclear option and only recommended when no other option is available) would be for you to put your education on a credit card or cards. However, let me preface by saying that unless you plan to either pay off the card during each semester or plan to immediately file for bankruptcy upon graduation, this is not a recommended option. What is recommended, is paying for adult education with a credit card versus a government-backed student loan, for the sole reason that if you are forced into bankruptcy, it will be possible to wipe the slate clean of all credit card debt, whereas with a student loan, that debt will not be removed. You can then plan on your wages being garnished for the foreseeable future.

Also, be advised that just because you graduated, that does not mean employers are lined up around the block to recruit you. Unless you choose a highly recruited field such as accounting, computer science, or engineering, your new degree may leave you in the same job that you worked at while you were in college. There are no guarantees you will be earning anywhere near the amount of money you require to pay off your college debt.

Consider your options, make a plan, and accomplish your goals. The best thing you can do in college is to hold yourself accountable.

Career Options Without Student loans

College is not for everyone, nor should it be. If your natural talents exist in an arena where other ways of learning are more conducive to you being personally successful, then why should you go to college? Go by your gut feeling, because it's usually right.

Individuals brought up within a successful family business should strongly consider taking it up due to the numerous pros. The first benefit to having someone else pave the way for you is that you don't have to incur any debt or financials stress. Your family has already covered the initial start-up costs and built the business, thus all you have to do is follow the same parameters. Secondly, because you're family, you're groomed for ownership. The business will be yours someday, and therefore you are trained to succeed. Even if you sometimes question your choice to pursue the family business due to a lack of independence, you can always pursue your own passion project on the side.

For individuals wanting to pursue a skilled trade career, such as an electrician, plumber, HVAC tech, etc., I recommend either paying for the schooling yourself or possibly with family assistance. Jobs are always available for skilled trades people, and can often lead directly into personal businesses, where you can be your own boss, and write off just about everything. The icing on the cake is that most skilled tradespeople acquire their skills without acquiring a boatload of debt along the way.

The military is always an option for those who qualify. Many who go into the military find their job and/or career extremely rewarding. They are given the chance to see the world, both the glamorous and not so glamorous sides of it. They are also given amazing benefits such as the G.I. Bill, which will pay for their college education as well as benefits toward insurance, food, housing, and retirement. For those without family or scholarship assistance, the military may be your best option. Whether you choose to pursue an active duty career or a part-time reserve, the numerous benefits to joining the military cannot be overlooked. Plus, you are personally doing your part to defend our country.

Other careers that simply require state licensing also exist, such as a real estate agent, insurance adjuster or agent, general contractor, roofer, etc. In order to work within any of these careers, most states will require that the individual pass a state exam and fulfill a continuing education requirement of a certain amount of credit hours, every two years or so. Once approved; however, the individual can begin their career immediately and without college debt. The only downside is that there may be significant start-up costs, depending on the career path.

Lines of Credit (Credit Card, Home Equity, Casino, etc.)

Attempting to manage credit card debt takes the ability to balance on a very slippery slope. Ideally, the best financial strategy for credit cards is to avoid them at all costs. Remember that the wealthy don't pay interest. Many of the offers that you will receive in the mail on a daily basis will try to persuade you by dangling carrots such as low cost balance transfers or 0% Annual Percentage Rate (APR) interest financing for the year. The credit card company knows they are not going to make money that first year, thus they are betting on you slipping up and running up a balance you cannot afford to pay off. The odds are weighted heavily against you and they know it. Also, the fine print will probably stat that the 0% APR, which was so appealing, is eventually going to balloon up to 18.99% or higher; great deal, or great Scott? Before you know it, you may need another card, to transfer the balance of your first card. God forbid you have a significant life event while trying to balance the cards. Remember that the wealthy wouldn't take that deal. The credit card companies make their offers as enticing as possible in hopes that you deviate from your plan. Don't fall for it.

I recommend having only one credit card for absolute emergencies. Forget the points, travel benefits, deals, rates, discounts, and any other credit card company selling pitch (such as the grand-daddy of them all – their stellar reputation). From now on, you will only have one card for use in emergency situations, such as when your debit card is not working and you don't have any cash.

It is easy to justify credit cards when you are not actively paying them back. Never charge more than you can afford to pay back on your following payday. Never.

Personal Loans

Personal loans are often easy to come by and are now more accessible than ever. Thanks to the Internet, peer-2-peer lending is readily available to anyone who applies. All you need to do is go to a website such as LendingClub.com or Prosper.com. Based on your credit history, as well as the amount, which you are hoping to loan, you will be categorized into a risk category with a corresponding interest rate. The higher risk you are, the higher the rate.

Personal loans through a bank may be available depending on your bank, while payday loan sharks are always available. If you really want to get hosed in a deal, go for a payday loan, where you could be facing an interest rate up to 50%! Payday loans from cash advance institutions should be avoided like the plague.

Personal loans from family members are also never a good idea. When money comes between family and friends it can fracture and even completely breakdown a relationship that was once healthy. Resentment builds between both parties about the daily payback. The person who took the loan will be complaining that the family member who gave the loan doesn't need the money anyway, while the other party feels awkward about asking for the money back. Don't go down this road, as it is far too easy for things to turn sour.

In conclusion, when it comes to personal loans, I would only recommended pursuing one in a debt consolidation scenario, where you are combining numerous high interest debts, such as credit cards, or medical bills in to a lower rate.

Payment Plans (Appliance, Electronics, Furniture, etc.)

It is far too easy today to fall into the trap of applying, qualifying, and receiving payment plans for various retail goods, such as appliances, electronics, and furniture. The plans are marketed as zero interest financing for a whole year! The retailers then justify that $2,000 TV you don't need, by selling you on the fact that it will only cost you $50 a month! Then, they reinforce the sales pitch by justifying the payment plan as allowing the buyer the opportunity to purchase an item or set of items that they otherwise couldn't afford, but now they can. Great deal! Right? Wrong.

The reality is that retail businesses make money by moving inventory, and in order to move unaffordable inventory, the retailers needed to get creative. Payment plans were a creation that I think directly correlates with the diminishing middle class.

What better way to suck in gullible buyers than with a low payment? Also, much like a credit card, retailers know the odds are against you for paying off the item within a year. If the odds were with you, you probably wouldn't have needed the payment plan in the first place. Therefore, it is in the best interest of the business to make passive income off of you.

Payment plans are marketed as a win-win, when in reality it is the customer who is losing. If you don't have the cash to purchase the item outright, taking a payment plan is like driving straight into a pothole and trying to justify it as just a little one. Regarding fundamentals, if you do not have the money to make the purchase outright, you are overextending yourself.

401(k) Retirement Plans

What do you really know about a 401(k) plan? When I was first exposed to a 401(k), all I knew was that it was a retirement account. I really didn't put much more stock into it than that. I knew I contributed a portion of my bi-weekly check, while my employer was supposed to contribute a match. I never put any thought into the servicer making money off of me. I also never really thought about the math-side of a 401(k), and whether this account could even support me. This is probably where most people are; they do what is popular, without asking why. For example, why does the government want me to contribute to a 401(k) plan? Or, why am I only allowed to contribute up to a certain point? Why should I pour all of my money outside of my other debts/bills, into a retirement account that I might never live to see?

The servicer has an interest in making money on your interest in a 401(k) account. Within my personal 401(k), the money is diversified into various types of mutual funds. Ironically though, they will not disclose how many shares I actually own within each fund – rather I'm just told the percentage of ownership. It is in the details where the servicer is making money on the interest, as well as billing fees on a quarterly or yearly basis. Additionally, many folks are often forced into an early distribution from a 401k due to inadequate savings or a significant life event. Well, guess who is there to tax the account? The government may not tax your 401k while you and your employer are depositing your salary and match into it; however, if you do take a distribution before you reach age 65, (which almost everyone does at some point) prepare to pay 30% of the distributed amount back in taxes. Per Bloomberg.com:

> The Internal Revenue Service collected 5.7 billion in 2011 from penalties, meaning that Americans took about

$57 billion from retirement funds before they were supposed to. The median size of a 401(k) is $24,400 as of March 31 (2014), with people older than 55 having $65,300, according to Fidelity Investments. Those funds can disappear quickly in retirement, and the early withdrawals indicate that the coming retirement crisis could be even more acute than expected. [12]

Speaking from experience, I am thirty-two, and I have around $20,000 in my 401(k) account, while my current yearly salary is over $80,000. So, doing the math, if I actually retired with even the $65,300 mentioned in the article, I would blow through that in about a year. So the question is, is a lifetime of savings worth it, for a year of salary at a point later in your life, which is not guaranteed? The numbers suggest that your 401(k) won't have anywhere near enough money to actually support you in retirement. Ultimately the retirement of your grandparents will be just that, unless you shoot for a career with either a pension or military retirement benefits.

Believe it or not, I am somewhat torn on the topic of 401(k) retirement plans. On one hand, your employer is offering free money (employer match), which you are leaving on the table if you don't invest. You are saying, "No thanks, I would rather not take your free money." On the other hand, you would be better served by investing into streams of passive income, focusing on a career with a pension, stock options, or joining the military reserve, in order to secure endless military retirement benefits. In addition, the system is rigged against you to favor the servicer and the government. The 401(k) sales pitch is built upon a false promise, that you even live to be sixty-five years of age.

If you have the extra money, a decent employer match (4% or more), and are also actively investing in alternative streams of passive income, I wouldn't discourage you from investing in a 401(k), because you never want to turn down free money. Unfortunately though, the reality is that very few are ahead of the game, and in a position to advance their personal finances, while actively contributing to a 401(k). You should also be cognizant that there are other investment options, which may be a better retirement plan (such as investing in property).

Our government, as well as your 401(k) servicer, can spin the sales pitch however they want to try and persuade you to invest; however, the proof is in the pudding. The actual results of the plan as a whole are mixed at best. Disbursements, taxes, and fees can decimate any account, just as easily as fluctuations in the stock market can wipe out years of investing. Ultimately, though, even if all of the stars align so that the stock market endlessly outperforms expectations year after year (which by the way, will never happen), and you never take a single disbursement while contributing to the account for your entire career, your account balance will never be able to support you long-term. Think twice about blindly investing in a 401(k) account, and ask yourself if a lifetime of questionable investment is truly worth a few years of security.

Our Story – The Student Loan Pothole

• **Situation** – I graduated in 2004 from the University of Central Florida with a Bachelor of Arts degree in Psychology. I graduated outside of the norm without debt, thanks to two scholarships, one paid by the state of Florida and the other by my father. I assumed that once I had obtained my Bachelor's degree, I would be highly marketable and recruited into the field of psychology. I assumed I would quickly obtain a job making somewhere around $30,000 a year. I went to summer school three out of four years and graduated in four years flat. A full year later I found myself fired from the valet company that I had worked for while I was in school for my psychology degree. I was never recruited by anyone in the field of psychology or mental health, and couldn't land a job to save my life. I was confused and bitter. I worked hard for that degree and was overqualified for a life as a valet attendant. I followed the valet firing by landing a job with the United States Postal Service (USPS) as a Rural Carrier (or mailman). I was a quick learner, and memorized routes quickly. Originally hired as part-time, before I knew it, I was working six days a week, or fulltime with overtime. I memorized eight different routes as well as came in at 3:30AM to work as a clerk and distribute pallets of magazines and commercial publications. I did everything the post office asked of me, and then some. Unfortunately, around the six-month mark, it became quite obvious that I was never going to move up in the post office because I wasn't a veteran of the military. Not knowing which way to turn, and feeling truly stuck, the only solution seemed to be to go back to school.

• **Task** – Learning my lesson from investing in a psychology career that never started, I chose to pursue a graduate degree in a field that I knew was always in high demand, and paid well – Management Information Systems (or a computer-related degree). Unfortunately, I didn't have the money to pay for my Master's degree, as I had no savings or employer benefits (as I was still technically a part-time employee). It should also be noted that Master's degree courses cost nearly triple the price of Bachelor's degree courses, thus I needed more money, which covered less schooling. Desperate to change my situation, the only option that was available was to take out a student loan. The application process seemed easy, and without consequence. I was in.

• **Action** – I applied and obtained $12,000 in government-backed student loans and started my first semester of graduate school.

• **Result** – Unlike my undergraduate degree, where I was able to work part-time around my school schedule, my graduate experience was the exact opposite. Due to the grind and long hours of my day job as a mailman, I was coming home at the end of each day physically exhausted. Studying, which at first was interesting, became more and more mundane. I was earning A's; however, I was becoming less and less interested. Eventually, I came to the conclusion that I couldn't see myself staring at a computer screen all day, thus computer programming wasn't going to be the answer. I dropped out toward the end of the first semester. I just quit in the middle. My A's turned to F's, and I completely burned the bridge with the school I was attending. I never obtained the graduate degree. What I did obtain though, was a $12,000 loan to repay, which I couldn't afford.

• **Takeaway** (or, lesson learned) – Nearly ten years later, I am still repaying this loan to the tune of $200 a month. I'm also not projected to pay it off until 2015, or a full ten years later.

The ramifications of a student loan can haunt you for years or even decades after the fact. I think it is also very easy to justify a new loan when you are not actively paying it back. There are some months that I could really use an additional $200, just for groceries. Obviously if I had to do it over again, I never would have taken that loan, because by taking the loan in the first place, I was overextending myself. During the times in the last ten years when I couldn't afford to repay the loan, the servicer "worked" with me to lower the payments, while my principal amount ballooned due to increased interest. Each year since taking out the loan I have paid in excess of $500 a year in interest, or a combined amount of about $5,000 in interest alone.

In summary, three things can be learned from the story above. One is that student loans are not the answer. There are various other ways to pay for school, which should be pursued prior. Number two is if you're experimenting with a new career path, never take out a loan (or over-commit yourself), or your personal finances will be paying the price for years to come. Ultimately, my student loan will not only cost me the $12,000 principal amount, but another $5,000 in interest, plus ten years of repayment, all for one semester toward I degree I did not obtain. Lastly, the number three reason to stay away from student loans is that even if you file for bankruptcy to wipe your slate clean of debt and start over, you cannot remove government-backed student loans. The government built the system to ensure they will always make their money back regardless of the false promise: that you will obtain a degree, plus a high-paying job to go with it.

Conclusion

Bad choices can and will cost you; therefore you need to be aware of the ramifications of your decisions. I fully endorse continuing your education and bettering your resume with an advanced degree; however, I do not recommend going into debt to accomplish it. Plain and simple, a loan or a line of credit is an overextension. If you do not have the money to buy what you want, you need to look to alternative methods and buy what you need. Exhibit resourcefulness, ask questions, research solutions, and adapt.

Money Tips

• Think about your upbringing and how your role models handle personal finance. What skills do they exhibit, and what lessons can you learn from them?

• If you need a personal loan to consolidate your debt, research lendingclub.com or prosper.com and see if it is possible to consolidate, while lowering your collective interest.

• If you're planning to better your education, start thinking about solutions for obtaining money for school that do not include borrowing money from the government.

• Try using the loan calculator on bankrate.com to better understand a loan.

• Explore finaid.org for more information on student loan forgiveness programs.

• Start thinking of alternative retirement options. Would you rather have a 401(k) with $65,000, or a rental house, worth $200,000, that pays you $1,400 a month in rent?

Timing

The time to take control of your finances is now. The earlier you start learning about personal finance, the better; however, it is never too late to start. Really, anytime is a good time, as it is never too late to secure your foundation.

Pre-Debt Stage

We will define the pre-debt stage as either young adulthood or adulthood without loan, credit, or personal debts. Within young adulthood, you have yet to experience many of the major life events that can bog down your personal finances. You have yet to bear the responsibility of supporting a family, children, marriage, financing a home, or vehicles. In this time, bills don't absorb the majority of your income. You are for the most part free of supporting others, and therefore able to save significant amounts of income toward major expenditures such as college, a home purchase, starting a personal business, etc. If, on the other hand, you find yourself as a full adult in the pre-debt stage, it is most likely because you have not had a significant life event occur. Another reason is that you have naturally steered your personal finances toward a specific outcome due to the influence of the support system around you. Call it conservative finances or call it luck; either way, take advantage of your circumstances, as nothing lasts forever.

Challenges within the Pre-Debt Stage

There are numerous potholes that someone within the pre-debt stage will need to navigate. Examples are (but not limited to the following):

• Peer Pressure – Peer influence is at its highest during young adulthood, when you are still trying to figure out who you are and where you fit in the world. You may not know if you want to go to college, join the military, pursue the family business, or start your own. You will be easily influenced if you have not received a financial education up to this point. In addition, many of your friends will be carelessly wasting their income at a time when they could be setting themselves up for years of success. Be your own person.

• Lack of experience – It is very hard to make a commitment to anything when you don't have the personal experience or confidence to support your plan. However, that is why I wrote this book, to share with you experience, insight, and provide the map. We will build your confidence.

• Lack of substantial income – You may not have scholarships or employer-paid college options available to you. Maybe a more natural choice is to choose to join the military. Or maybe you would be a better fit as a licensed real estate or insurance agent. Another possibility is that you don't have the money for advanced schooling, but do have an easily accessible family business. Go with your gut, and do what feels best for you. I cannot tell you which path is best for you personally, but rather give you the map that avoids potholes. There are certain life and career paths that encounter substantially less friction than others, and therefore may be a more natural fit. I make my recommendations based upon my own research and personal experience.

• Lack of support – When you start to differ from the path that your parents took, you're going to run into friction. They might take your new direction as a knock against their strategy, or they may discount you by stating that because you don't have the experience you don't know what you're talking about. The way I would approach the situation is by explaining that you value their opinion and still want them to be a part of your support system, but that you have formulated your own you will be making your own adult decisions.

Opportunities to Take Advantage of within the Pre-Debt Stage

Individuals in the pre-debt stage should take advantage of the following opportunities or options within their personal finance planning:

• Mobility – Young adulthood is one of the best times of your life to be mobile. It is a time where you have yet to be locked into a location due to family or job responsibilities. Additionally, there are a lot of opportunities out there in careers, which require travel. Whether in the business, insurance or the travel industry, being mobile is preferred by most employers – especially those, which promote employees who do stints at their home office location.

• College – Your goal for college should be to graduate debt free. The way to do this is to attain scholarships, part-time employment, save your money, or join the military (for access to the GI Bill). Do not assume that your family will support you. Do not place college on a credit card or personal loan, and never apply for a government-backed student loan. Remember that government-backed student loans are the ultimate worst loan you could ever take, as even in post-bankruptcy, you will still owe the full outstanding balance of the loan(s).

• Military – The military is an excellent option for anyone, especially those who are coming from a lower-income family, those with a history of service, or those without the resources to pay for advanced education (college, trade schools, licensing courses, etc. Within the military you will become an adult and held accountable. There are numerous great advantages to joining the military such as the GI Bill (where the military will pay for your college), VA Home Loans, Health Insurance, Free Rent (!), Commissary access (discounted groceries), military retirement benefits after twenty years of service, camaraderie, travel, etc. From my personal experience, I somewhat regret not having joined the military, due to the numerous benefits I am currently missing out on. The GI bill alone could have saved me from my current student loan, and when I think about military retirement income on top of social security, as well as a pension, we're talking about potentially being set for the rest of your life versus any type of retirement struggle.

• Home Purchase Preparation – Young adulthood is a great time to save as much money as possible toward the purchase of a home. Home loans and especially first time home-buyers can get taken advantage of royally by loan officers and the first-time home-buyer loan products being marketed to them. Buying a home for $200,000 with a 3% down payment, you can plan on spending another $200,000 in interest over the life of that loan, unless you either pay biweekly or run into a windfall. Your only other option is to contribute significant additional principal with each payment. If you find yourself placed with an FHA (or government-backed) loan as your only option, you would honestly be better off continuing to rent. FHA rules place the homebuyer in a firm disadvantage, and should be avoided if at all possible.

• Purchasing a car – Make sure that any car purchase you make is for a vehicle that is at least five years old (if not older), due to the constantly depreciating value of the asset. It has been said that the moment you drive a new car off the dealer's lot, it instantly loses value. Dave Ramsey has stated that within the first four years a car will lose 60% of its value [13]. Regardless of the expert, do yourself a favor and don't overpay for a depreciating asset. Make sure that your next car purchase is used, and that you buy it with cash. Financing is not recommended, and again would be overextending yourself by spending money that you do not have, under the false assumption that in the future you will have it. Take advantage of this time of your life and buy your car in full, with cash.

• Weddings – I highly recommend close destination weddings with a limited gathering of friends/family. You can always follow-up a destination wedding with a party at your house or another convenient location. The cost of big weddings today can range anywhere from $25,000 - $100,000 and up. I assure you that if you are planning a big wedding, that the cost per guest, cost to reserve the place of the wedding, flowers, music (DJ, orchestra, band), food, clothing, photography, cake, wedding planner, etc., can easily blow your budget right out of the water, as costs quickly get out of hand with each family member or friend's requests and recommendations. Stay well under budget and choose a destination. Not only will you avoid the separate cost of a honeymoon (because you're already there), but you'll also avoid all the other costs for a fraction of the price.

• Children – Complete school, start your career, purchase a home, and remove all debt prior to starting a family. Having children is one of the best things that can ever happen you, and a truly amazing and humbling experience; however, you owe it to your kids to be prepared so that you can fully support them. You are their role model, and will need to set the example for personal finance for them. They will love you unconditionally in the process.

Present-Debt Stage

If you're already well into adulthood with multiple debts/bills, well you're not alone. Very few adults are actually debt free and typically those that are debt free are only that way because they hit rock bottom at some point, learned the error of their ways, and turned things around. The vast majority of everyone else drives new cars, lives in large, oversized houses, throw their daily expenditures on credit cards (in hopes of earning points), and have a mountain of debt to go with it. Often, those who project that they have money are the same people who flutter through their various credit cards just to find one, which isn't maxed out, in order to pay for their country club membership. Things sure are shiny on the surface, but under the hood, the engine is out of oil. You don't want to drive this clunker.

Challenges within the Present-Debt Stage

There is no perfect time to fix a flat tire, but has to be done for your car to get back on the road and take you where you need to go. Time is like the treads of your tires; the older you get, the more tread you lose. Take advantage of timing before your tires go bald, because these tires you can't replace. With middle-aged and older adults, timing presents some very unique challenges:

• Taking care of others/responsibility – Typically, the older you get, the more responsibility you naturally tend to take on. Grown adults have family responsibilities to take care of children, elderly parents, relatives, pets, friends, and anyone else. With each party you take care of, you may be directly or indirectly financing the care, and as we well know, taking care of others is expensive.

• Experience – In middle age you know what you like and what you don't, based upon personal experience. Unfortunately, what you like is not always good for you. Everyone has a vice, whether it be a new house, car, truck, boat, hot tub, swimming pool, alcohol, cigarettes, season tickets, motorcycles, etc. What you like is going to cost you, at the expense of paying off your debt.

• Outstanding Debts – You may be at the point in your life that you've acquired so many debts that you've completely lost control of managing them. Loan, credit and personal debts over a lifetime of bad personal financial decisions can be overwhelming and demoralizing. Your personal finances are the elephant in the room, and you very well may have created the world's largest elephant. However, like the old saying goes, "the only way to eat an elephant is one bite at a time." With that, you may be eating for quite a while.

• Time – You may feel that you naturally just do not have the tread left on the tires to attempt to get the land of financial freedom and live the debt free life you have always dreamed of. What you may not realize though, is that as long as you're alive there is hope. Unfortunately, many choose this crutch as the reason why they cannot be fiscally responsible, which in my opinion is a cop-out.

• Physical impairment – You may be disabled or on a fixed income and therefore do not venture out and coincidently miss out on opportunities. With today's technology however, it is totally possible for someone to work from his or her home and start an Internet business, work as a consultant, or work as a personal assistant.

• You're stuck in the past (over a missed opportunity) – Because you're blinded by a past mistake you may be missing fresh opportunities on a regular basis. Get over the past and look toward the future. Re-energize yourself, and make a deliberate effort to push past the boundary.

• Lack of confidence – Maybe your life has not worked out quite as you thought it would. Or, due to a traumatic life event, your plans dramatically changed for the worse, and you've never quite recovered. Once again though, as long as you are alive, it is never a bad time to better yourself, your personal finances, and your life. One word comes to mind; try.

Opportunities to Take Advantage of within the Present-Debt Stage

Believe it or not, there are many advantages to paying down debt as a middle-aged or older adult. Some examples are:

• Higher income – Many middle-aged or older adults make more if not significantly more income than they did as young adults, whether it be earned, unearned, or portfolio income. Put that additional income toward your debts first and wants second.

• Experience – At this point in your life, you know where you've been and you have a pretty good idea of where you want to go. You're experienced in large purchases, life events, and tax season. With your combined knowledge you are more likely to follow through and accomplish your goals than ever before.

• You are an adult – There's no more room for excuses at this point in your life. It is time for you to step up and fulfill the potential which you always knew was there. You can't blame anyone else anymore. Look in the mirror, accept that you've driven through potholes, and move forward with your new map, and new life.

• You are a role model – Motivate yourself to be a role model to your children, nieces, nephews, friends and extended family by proving what you can do with an education in personal finance.

• The big picture – You are ready to work to live rather than live to work. Your perspective is greater as you focus on family gatherings, significant life events, and even vacations. Be prepared and live your life to the fullest. *Pura Vida!*

Our Story – The Missed Timing Pothole

• **Situation** – We didn't realize how badly we were in debt until I stopped my traveling day job as a field catastrophe claims adjuster. Once I got off the road and went into the office, the immediate pay cut was somewhere in the ballpark of $30,000. We instantly went from living large, where I made quick thousands, to falling into the red, going further into debt each month. We were unprepared and had never adequately planned for how to financially deal with such a pay cut. We were badly over-extended. Around the same time, one of my good friends who was the same age—a co-worker with the same company, in the exact same position, and my next-door neighbor—was not only living debt free, but well on his way to paying off his house. I never realized how far ahead of me he was until it finally sank in how far behind we were. Before we could move ahead; however, we needed to take a good look into the past.

• **Task** – Analyze our past choices and financial decision-making. Find out how our neighbor planned and conservatively invested in his personal finances in order to come out debt free.

• **Action** – After comparing our situations, a trend began to emerge that even though we both made big money in the field, my buddy was investing his money into his debts, while I was wasting ours day trading, buying a sports car, and purchasing a home with an insufficient down payment. He had saved up and put down $40,000 toward a $200,000 home, paid off his entire student loan balance, and continued to pay extra toward his home with each payday. He never purchased a car and continued to drive his company van only. He didn't mess with the stock market or any other get rich quick schemes and instead invested conservatively. He also paid off, shredded, and closed all of his credit cards.

• **Result** – Today this same friend is 100% debt free. His $200,000 home is completely paid off. He and his wife own both of their cars in full, the newest purchased completely with cash. Neither one of them has student loan debt, credit card debt, or personal loan debt. They have no revolving lines of credit, pay no interest, live debt-free, and go on sweet vacations. For their honeymoon they not only decided to go to Oktoberfest in Munich, Germany, but also went to Italy and San Juan, Puerto Rico, all in the same trip. They've also gone to Hawaii, in addition to other places. My buddy now puts his money into various investment accounts, while also contributing a full 8% of his salary into his 401(k), which is matched at 100%. He is way ahead of the game and ahead of us.

• **Takeaway** – I invested into the stock market riding the highs and lows of day trading when I could have been paying off my student loans. I also could have been paying off our home when I was instead wasting money putting exhaust, headers, stereo equipment, etc. into my sports car. That same car I sold shortly after our son was born because it was too small. Also, when I still owned the car, I rarely drove it, as my company car had free gas and maintenance. The sports car took super unleaded, and was more of a chore to drive than fun. I realized that I placed our family at a huge disadvantage by not preparing for children. Children cost a lot of money and can easily take up much of your income, thus the time prior to our son being born, would have been perfect for a financial tune-up, setting ourselves up for the future. Unfortunately at the time, I didn't realize we had a problem, and therefore I drove straight into *The Missed Timing Pothole*.

Conclusion

Timing can be your greatest asset if you work it in your favor. There is always time to improve your personal finances, but certain times in your life are definitely more advantageous for different reasons. I would highly recommend that you analyze your own situation and begin to map out what you can take advantage of with timing in your life, and how that may be able to impact your personal finances. Remember that the best time to invest is now, by investing in you first. Pay off your debts.

Money Tips

• Write down personal finance opportunities for you to take advantage of as well as familiarize yourself with challenges.

• Take advantage of timing by planning and preparing for significant life events.

• Make it your mission to pay off your debts, while continuing your daily life.

• Pursue a debt-free education. Be cognizant that college is a critical time, where it is very easy to fall into debt, due to the justification that you are only overextending yourself now, and that once you graduate you will be entitles to a job.

ASSESSMENT

Now that we've discussed the framework for wealth and awareness, it is time to assess your own personal finances. This is the point in the book, where you look into the mirror and accept responsibility for your personal finances, whether you made poor decisions or life gave you lemons. It is time to take ownership and analyze where you are, and where you want to go.

<u>The Starting Line Concept</u>

The concept of the starting line came to me at random, much like the interest epiphany. I was contemplating our finances and analyzing the finances of the wealthy. The more I looked at the finances of the wealthy a trend started to emerge: the majority of those who were wealthy didn't start their adult lives in debt. From there, I began to look at debt as a delay, whereas no debt meant no delays. Imagine that you're in your personal finance vehicle at the starting line with all of your peers. Everyone is revving the gas as the lights change from red to yellow to green. When the light goes green however, all of your peers, friends, and family take off, while your car isn't allowed to start yet, but forced to wait. The more time goes by, the further ahead the competition is, and the further behind you fall. The more debt you have, the longer the wait. Before you know it, the competition has already made multiple trips around the track and you haven't even hit the gas yet. This is how the wealthy stay rich, while the rest of us never even start the race.

Student loan debt, which we covered in the prior chapter, is one of the top reasons for delaying your start. With the average student loan debt approaching $30,000, many young adults are finding themselves saddled with debt for next ten to twenty years post-graduation. Try to also imagine applying for and receiving additional school loans to cover the costs of a graduate or doctorate degree (especially in a field like medicine or law). The amount of your student loan debt could easily top $100,000. Per the loan calculator on finaid.org, a $100,000 student loan with a 6.8% interest rate would equal a loan repayment amount of $1,150.80 a month for ten years! That's more than most mortgage payments! Even more flabbergasting is that the cumulative interest paid on the life of this loan would exceed $38,000.

The reality of student loans is that they're sold with a false promise that you will be given a job, based upon your degree, which will pay enough to not only cover the repayment of your student loans, but also pay for all of your other personal bills outside of the loan.

That cart is way ahead of the horse. Once you attain your degree, you may never even go into the field in which you attained your degree. You will not be given a job just because you graduated or attended a school with a great reputation. Even an internship is not a sure thing. Unless you had a college internship for one to two years prior to graduation with a company that now truly wants you, your options may be dwindling. In reality, there are no employers waiting for you and there will be no handouts. You will apply to jobs all day, every day, and continuously be rejected for anything and everything because you have no formal job experience in the field.

If you do happen to land a job from a job fair, Internet posting, or through a friend, the odds that it will pay enough to offset your student loan debt are severely against you. You may be able to somehow pay your loan payment, but good luck saving for a home, car, vacation, or any other life event or big purchase. If you are unable to pay your loan, you can always go on deferment for a year or two while the principal balance balloons out of control. Is it becoming obvious why student loans can cause you to lose the race?

All types of debt, including credit card, personal and student loans, are an overextension and detrimental to your race results. Do you want to take off when the light goes green or sit in idle while the cars around you continue to lap your stalled car? I know the answer and so do you.

Financial Snapshot – Phase 1

The best way to assess your finances is with one question: are you overhead free? If the answer is no, you've got some analyzing to do. If the answer is yes, then either you have been lucky and indirectly learned how to manage your personal finances conservatively, or you just haven't hit that big pothole yet where the bottom fell out.

Speaking from our experience, I never truly grasped how poor our personal finances were until we started tracking them. In our first chart I created a budget. Then I expanded the chart to track each of our debts with the correlating interest rates. I eventually added our salaries and potential savings, as well as our bills-to-income ratio. Seeing our financial picture for the first time was like taking a towel and wiping off our fogged up windshield. Suddenly we could see where we were paying the greatest amount of interest and which debts were costing us the most. We could see how much money we had available each paycheck after paying bills, which we could now allocate toward debt. We were also able to roughly time out how long it was going to take to pay off the debt. When we made the decision that we were going to live credit-free, we decided we needed to keep an emergency fund at all times, to float us through any potential emergencies or unplanned life events. Adding the emergency fund category to our chart at zero was an instant eye-opener of how bad our finances were. I followed that by adding a college fund for our son, which was also at zero. Unfortunately, the zeros in our financial picture were not after numbers, but rather all by themselves.

Future Finances – Phase 2

The second phase of your financial assessment is to map out your future. What goals do you have in mind or would you like to accomplish? Start by setting daily goals, and become mindful of everyday circumstances where you could save money. Follow your daily goals with weekly goals or bi-weekly goals depending on your pay cycle. Eventually build up to monthly goals and yearly goals. Where do you see yourself in one year, two years, five years, or ten years? Which debt would you feel the most proud of to pay off? Are you saddled with a large house, car, credit, or student loan debt? Do you have debt so large that it currently feels like an elephant in the backseat of your personal finance vehicle? Allocate money in your budget for the items that are most important to you. Are you a traveler of the world? Or maybe you enjoy taking cruises. Is your hobby cars, home improvement, or season tickets to sporting events? You can make your goals a reality if you budget, plan, and execute when the time is right. How many times have you received coupons for items that you need to buy, but don't have the money to actually use them? Or maybe you just completely missed a great buy one-get one (bogo) deal at the grocery store because it unfortunately fell during your off week. Start allocating the money now so that when opportunities arise, you can strike.

Every day we are brainwashed to think that a magical windfall will just drop out of the sky into our lap, due to the constant pop culture marketing showing us lives of luxury and excess. In reality, $100,000 weddings are just plain absurd, while home shows displaying new homebuyers with a budget of $400,000 - $800,000 are completely ridiculous. I remember one episode, where one member of the couple was a teacher, while the other was unemployed. Somehow they magically had a new home budget, which exceeded $700,000. So, either they had just robbed the bank down the street, or they raided funds from the bank of mom and dad, living off of old family money, or they have a very risky line of credit.

In the real world, there are no handouts and no guarantees. In order for you to beat the system and accomplish your goals independently, you must plan for a life free of overhead. When opportunities present themselves, you take the exit and capitalize.

Our Story – The "Driving Blind" Pothole

• **Situation** – We didn't realize we were driving blind until the pay cut I received when I left my traveling job. Suddenly each and every debt mattered for the first time and we were forced to assess our finances. We had various doctor bills; home services such as security, pest control, and lawn maintenance; numerous credit card debts; four student loans between us totaling more than $30,000; and additional unnecessary debts and bills. We had been driving blind for so long that we pretty much drove into a sinkhole, which was going to take years to climb out of.

• **Task** – Get rid of the debt.

• **Action** – The first step we took was to begin steadily paying off each debt, smallest to largest. We downsized our phone plans and insurance policies. We continued to pay off our doctor bills and made a push at our student loans. I cancelled our home security, lawn mowing, and pest control services. We figured that now that I was going to be home, I take care of the lawn, while the security system we never used anyway. Grand total we had spent $3,000 - $4,000 on the security service alone after upgrading our outdated system and unknowingly signing up for their unbreakable three-year contract. Upon finishing the install, the installer flew through the terms as he was trying to be done for the day. I never read the fine print and just signed the contract so he could be on his way. At the end of the contract, we would have been better off having all of our stuff stolen and filing a claim under our homeowner's policy.

• **Result** – Along with the lesson learned from signing a bad contract, with each bit of extra money we had available, we began to pay off our debts.

• **Takeaway** – We will never go back to driving blind ever again. Much like someone with a drug problem or someone else in a bad relationship, it is very difficult to realize the magnitude of the problem when you're in the middle of it. Once we officially started our plan, we turned the page on that chapter of our lives. Currently we are still paying a few of our larger debts, mainly the student loans; however, the remainders of the rest of our debts have been completely removed.

Conclusion

Like driving at midnight without your headlights on, this is how many people are currently navigating personal finance. They hit whatever is in the road. Plowing through potholes, the vast majority of our society is driving clunkers. Are you driving blind? You need to assess your finances and write them down. Include your debts as well as your goals. If one of your goals is to save up for a vacation, add a vacation category, even if you don't currently have any savings. Staring at the zero on a regular basis will motivate you to change that number. The same concept can be applied to your personal savings as well as a college fund for your kids (if you have kids). Knowing you are behind is a great motivator to make a change.

Money Tips

• Apply the Starting-Line Concept to your life. If you aren't living overhead free, then you're not in the race.

• Write down your finances. Write out each debt amount and when you project to pay it off.

• Write down each savings goal. If you don't have the money to start the goal, list it at zero. Motivate yourself.

DEBT MANAGEMENT

You don't go into debt overnight and you don't get out of debt overnight. Going into debt is usually the culmination of years of bad financial decisions (or potholes), that one by one have added up to leave you with a clunker of a personal finance vehicle. Correct your finances moving forward, with years of good financial decisions. Start with sound debt management strategies and track your progress. Much like someone trying to lose weight by counting their calories, if you really want to lose debts, you need to track them.

Debt Management Concepts

Personal finances can easily be convoluted after years of driving blind, thus the first part to debt management is organization. You need to be able to know what you are working with so you know where to start. Think of debt like the pieces in a chess set. You have no idea what move to make when they're still in the box. You have to set them up on the board, moving one piece at a time, until you accomplish your goal of checkmating debt.

Concept 1. **The Debt Snowball**

The best way that I have found to pay down debt is with the debt snowball. So, what exactly is the debt snowball? The debt snowball is a system for paying off debt by paying the minimum on each of your debts except for one. The lone debt that you are not paying the minimum on, you absolutely hammer with as much money as possible. The concept itself is very simple and anyone can do it. Variations however, play into the debt snowball concept, and should be implemented based on your own personal finances.

Some experts recommend paying off the smallest debt first, while others recommend paying the debt with the highest interest rate first. I like to consider the tax implication as well. You cannot write off credit card or car loan debt; however, you can write off student and home loan debt. Therefore, you need to assess your debts and decide which strategy works best for you. Personally, we pay the lowest debt first, while also focusing on the tax implication. You may decide that focusing on the highest interest debt first makes the most sense to you due to the amount of the balance. Really there are pros and cons with each option.

In summary, the debt snowball is a great option for anyone looking to get his or her personal finance vehicle back in the race. I highly recommend the debt snowball to anyone who is just starting his or her own debt management.

Concept 2. **The 50/50 Rule**

The concept of the 50/50 Rule is to aim for 50% or less of your take home (net) income going toward bills/debts. Having lived with and without money, I firmly believe that your total percentage of net monthly income to bills should never be more than 50%, and by all means be as far below 50% as possible. Anything greater than 50% and you really start to feel the financial pinch, where you are no longer able to do the things you want to do when you want to do them. It's also very easy to overextend yourself when you're not tracking the percentage, which is why I highly recommend tracking it. By following the percentage on a regular basis you can see whether you are paying too much for certain bills. You will also be able to see the percentage fall as your debts begin to drop off, which can really give you momentum. On the other hand, if your personal finances are within the parameters of the 50/50 Rule, and you haven't been actively tracking it, then count yourself lucky and start tracking it today.

Afford your wants as well as your needs, and start living the life you should by embracing the 50/50 Rule. If you currently spend more than half of your take-home income on bills, then this is a wake-up call that you are driving a real jalopy of a personal finance vehicle. It's time to start taking care of your ride.

Debt Management Tools

It is 100% true that you can do anything with the right tools. It is also 100% true that without the right tools you can be at a serious disadvantage, especially when it comes to accomplishing financial goals. Think of an auto mechanic trying to repair a car without the proper socket wrench or pneumatic air gun. Not only would it be increasingly frustrating, but it would also take significantly more effort and time to accomplish a task that could be quick and easy. To this point, I like to use specific tools in our daily debt management that have made quite an impact and become very helpful in clearing up our own personal finances.

Tool 1. Bill Schedule/Budget

The first tool I created was a Bill Schedule/Budget. Within the schedule, I list the frequency (date or recurring date of the bill), name of the bill itself, the amount, and whether it is set to auto-pay or not. A miscellaneous category is added for items such as dentist/doctor bills and auto maintenance. The bills listed are then separated based upon whether the bill due date is in the first payday of the month or the second. Recurring bills for each payday such as groceries and gasoline are listed in both sections. At the bottom of the chart I like to list Net Bi-Weekly Salary, Net Yearly Salary (bonuses included in the calculation), Net Salary Less Bills for each biweekly payday and the Percentage of Monthly Net Income that Goes to Bills. The last figure is for the 50/50 Rule, and similar to a Debt-to-Income ratio, with the exception that rather than focusing on gross income, we are concerned with Net Income. See Figure 1 for example:

Figure 1.

Bill Schedule/Budget			
Frequency	Bills	Amount	Auto Pay
Bi-Weekly	House Payment	$575.00	No
1st	Auto Insurance	$160.00	Yes
13th	Gas (House)	$33.00	No
13th	Cell Phone	$125.00	No
1st - 15th	Groceries	$300.00	No
1st - 15th	Gas (Auto)	$100.00	No
Bi-Weekly	House Payment	$575.00	No
19th	Utilities	$250.00	No
24th	Car Payment	$225.00	No
26th	TV	$67.00	No
28th	Student Loan Repayment	$175.00	No
29th	Internet	$45.00	No
15th - 31st	Groceries	$300.00	No
15th - 31st	Gas (Auto)	$100.00	No
Miscellaneous Bills			
Frequency	Bills	Amount	Auto Pay
Per Visit	Physical/Occupational Therapy	$35.00	Yes
Per Visit	Dentist	$50.00-$100.00	No
Per Visit	Auto Maintenance	TBD	No
Net Salary - 2 weeks $2,700.00		Salary Less Bills 1st-15th $1,407.00	
Yearly Net Salary $72,764.47		Salary Less Bills 16th - 31st $963.00	
% of Monthly Income that goes to Bills 49.97%			

By having each of your bills written out, you will know where you have extra money and where you do not. It is also very helpful for planning. With the example above, you would have significantly more income during the first pay day of the month versus the second. You could decide to leave your budget somewhat lopsided, thus one pay day feels like more of a bonus than the other, or you could always move a bill or two from the second bi-weekly payment period to the first to create a more balanced budget.

Tool 2. **Debt Snowball Chart**

Following the Bill Schedule/Budget is the Debt Snowball Chart complete with debt totals. Within the Debt Snowball Chart is where you will capture each of your debts (ranked lowest to highest). For each debt, list the name of the debt, balance, and interest rate. Just below the Debt Snowball Chart, I like to capture: Total Debt (Less House), Outstanding Accounts, Total Credit Card Debt, Total Monthly Bills, Total Student Loan Debt, Total Student Loan 1 Debt (this category adds Student Loan 1A and 1B), Total Debt (Less House), Total House Debt, Yearly Interest on Combined Debt, and Yearly Interest on House Debt. Each category is essentially based on the debt snowball table above, and with the input of a few simple excel formulas, the chart will calculate itself automatically. With each payment that you make toward each debt within the top of the chart, the fields located in the bottom will auto-calculate the change. See Figure 2.

Figure 2.

Debt Snowball Chart		
Debt:	Amount Owed:	Interest Rate:
Student Loan 1A	$2,600.00	4.13%
Student Loan 1B	$1,400.00	4.13%
Credit Card 1	$4,900.00	7.90%
Auto Loan	$7,800.00	2.69%
Student Loan 2	$15,500.00	6.80%
Home Loan	$162,000.00	4.625%
Total Debt (Less House)	Outstanding Accounts	
$32,200.00	6	
Total Combined Credit Card Debt	Total Monthly Bills	
$4,900.00	$3,030.00	
Total Student Loan Debt	Total Student Loan 1 Debt	
$19,500.00	$4,000.00	
Total Debt (Less House)	Total House Debt	
$32,200.00	$162,000.00	
Yearly Interest on Combined Debt	Yearly Interest on House Debt	
$1,815.99	$7,492.50	

Tool 3. Savings

The last category to efficiently capture is going to be savings. Now, savings does not represent savings in just a savings account alone, but rather any type of income that is left over after your bills have been paid. Within the Savings category I like to capture: Total Savings Per Month, Total Savings Per Year, Total Savings Per Five Years, Total Savings Per Ten Years, Emergency Fund, and Kid's College Fund. Keep in mind that there are many other categories for saving, which you could add to your own chart. The categories I capture are merely the ones that I like to focus on. See Figure 3.

Figure 3.

Savings
Total Savings Per Month
$2,370.00
Total Savings Per Year
$36,404.47
Total Savings Per 5 Years
$182,022.35
Total Savings Per 10 Years
$364,044.70
Emergency Fund
$2,500.00
Kid's College Fund
$0.00

Notice that the within the Savings chart that Kid's College fund is listed at $0.00 and color-coded in red. I highly recommend adding savings categories even if they are at zero because they spotlight areas of your personal finances that need attention. Also, I like to color-code insufficient amounts or debts in red to provide emphasis that this category warrants a correction on your part. Each time you place emphasis on areas that you need to improve upon, it will only aid to cleanup your financial picture.

Financial Statement

It is important that you understand that a financial statement incorporates three areas of finance: a balance sheet, income statement, and statement of cash flows. According to Wikipedia (2014, para. 1-2), "a financial statement (or financial report) is a formal record of the financial activities of the business, person, or other entity. Relevant financial information is presented in a structured manner and in a form easy to understand."[14] For the sake of your personal finances, there is going to be some overlap. I have personally found that the formality of the three sections of a financial report are not completely necessary for the average person, as they are better tailored to apply to a business. Therefore, I prefer to focus on tracking my balance sheet, debts, net income, and savings, and let apps track the rest (which encompasses the financial statement and statement of cash flows).

Balance Sheet

Assets and Liabilities are the two main categories, which comprise your Balances Sheet. Assets less Liabilities equals Net Worth, is what you are going to track. See Figures 4 – 6, for an example of a Balance Sheet.

Figure 4.

Assets			
Cash & Cash Equivalents		Property	
Cash on hand		Primary Residence	225000.00
Checking accounts	500.00	Secondary Residence	
Savings Accounts	2500.00	Rental Property	
Money Markets		Investment Property	
Certificates of deposit		Vehicle 1	7250.00
Other		Vehicle 2	4700.00
Total Cash & Cash Equivalents	$ 3,000.00	Total Property	$ 236,950.00
Brokerage Accounts		Other Assets	
Stocks		Other	
Mutual Funds		Life insurance cash surrender value	
Municipal Bonds		Jewelry	15500.00
Corporate Bonds		Furnishings	50000.00
Commodities		Peer-2-Peer Lending	
Total Brokerage Accounts	$ -	Digital Property (Ebooks)	
Retirement Accounts		Musical Instruments	5500.00
401(A)	9500.00	Computers	2500.00
457(B)	7500.00	Total Other Assets	$ 73,500.00
401(K)		Total Assets	$ 416,290.80
IRA - Roth			
IRA - Traditional			
Profit Sharing			
Pension	85840.80		
Total Retirement Accounts	$ 102,840.80		

Figure 5.

Liabilities		
Short-Term Credit		
Credit Card 1		4900
Credit Card 2		
Credit Card 3		
Loans from friends/family		
Home line of credit		
Other		
Total Short-Term Credit	$	4,900.00
Loans & Mortgages		
Primary Residence		160000
Secondary Residence		
Rental Property		
Investment Property		
Vehicle 1		7800
Student Loan 1		4000
Student Loan 2		15500
Business Loan		
401(A) Loan		
Total Loans & Mortgages	$	187,300.00
Other Liabilities		
Other 1		
Other 2		
Total Other Liabilities	$	-
Total Liabilities		$ 192,200.00

Figure 6.

Current Net Worth	$ 224,090.80
Net Worth Projection	
2014	$ 224,090.80
2015	$ 235,295.34
2016	$ 247,060.11
2017	$ 259,413.11
2018	$ 272,383.77

Income Statement/Statement of Cash flows

For your income statement and statement of cash flows, I prefer to use apps due to their ease of tracking, record keeping, and reporting. I have personally found that trying to track each expenditure myself through excel was not only mind numbing, but also consumed a ridiculous amount of time. Apps are a great solution.

One of the best apps that I have found is the free app/website offered by Mint.com. Within Mint (which you can access either through their website, your phone, or tablet), you can add each of your accounts categorized by cash, credit cards, loans, investments, and property. They also track trends and have various charts and graphs for your monthly expenditures. You are able to build budgets and goals. Mint will also email you weekly regarding expenditures, goal progress, summaries, etc. I like it for its ease of use and appealing design. It is very easy to understand and seamlessly covers the essentials of your income statement.

Outside of Mint, there are plenty of other budget sites/apps, which are available with a simple download or registration. For tracking bills, I like to use Check, which give you the ability to auto-pay your bills as well as track your accounts. You can even track your hotel and airline points, which Mint does not capture. Due to the differences between the two, Intuit, which owns Mint, purchased Check.

Additional Resources

In order to properly repair your personal finance vehicle from all of those years of potholes, you need to become resourceful. Luckily, there are all kinds of resources that are readily available to assist you on your financial journey. Websites, calculators, programs, blogs/libraries of information, books, webinars, radio shows, podcasts, classes, and various other options are available to anyone who is looking for them. For the sake of this book I am going to focus on the ones that I have found made the greatest impact.

Microsoft Excel should be one of the number one tools on your buy list for cleaning up your personal finances. The charts I created above were made in Excel and I use them on a daily basis. If you are unfamiliar with Excel, I recommend either taking an Excel class or learning Excel from a website like Youtube.com. There are numerous experts on Youtube.com that can show you how to perform just about any function that Excel offers, including formulas. Thus, even those who are not as technically savvy can learn Excel with ease.

There are also numerous financial websites that I visit regularly for assistance with personal finance. Bankrate.com is great for calculators such as a mortgage or car loan pay off calculator. Investopedia.com has tons of information on investing. Marketwatch.com, Motleyfool.com, DailyFinance.com, Yahoo Finance, or IHub.com, are all great resources for stock market research. If you really enjoy learning about daily finance with simple articles, the Mint Life Blog is an excellent resource. Biggerpockets.com is a great site for anyone looking to get into rental properties. Overall there are lots and lots of popular as well as start-up finance websites available at your disposal.

What would a financial journey be without the inspiration provided by some of the world's greatest experts? Start going to your local bookstore or EBook store, and browse the finance section. There are all kinds of financial experts from all walks of life who can each offer you a different perspective on finance. Various financial gurus can also be found on podcast and radio shows.

The only caution I would mention is to be mindful in your research that not every article written offers good financial advice. For example, articles on how to improve your credit score are missing the mark entirely. They're focusing on appeasing creditors by keeping you in debt. Another example of poor financial advice can be found in articles that list all of the easy ways you can pay down debt. First of all, there is no easy way to pay down debt. Sinking your paycheck into a black hole every two weeks is not sexy, nor easy. Paying off debt is a means to an end. Giving you the false hope that you can depend on a windfall is not only a farce, but also ridiculous, as it does not apply to everyone. Lots of other pieces of poor advice can be found on student loans in particular, which talk up the benefits of student loans, including deferment and student loan forgiveness. Don't drink the Kool-Aid. Sift through the bunk advice, and pull out the good.

Our Story – Wasted Opportunity – The Sports Car Pothole

• **Situation** – Within two years after graduating college, I landed my first big job. I had a few bills such as my graduate student loan, but other than that, I had no worries. So, naturally, rather than pay off the student loan, I spent my money on other things. As travel was 75% of my job, I had a lot of money and nothing fun to spend it on. Right around this same time, one of my best friends (who also had a good job, but was making a fraction of my salary and still living it home) decided to buy a sports car. He picked up an orange Ford Mustang GT that roared. The car was awesome. I on the other hand had a company car that hauled a ladder and was full of carpet samples.

• **Task** – I decided I too needed a sports car.

• **Action** – I purchased a 2006 Nissan 350Z that I had been eyeing for quite a few years. My new car payments were around $475 a month. The car also took Super Unleaded, which I justified as the price of owning a sports car.

• **Result** – My buddy and I each had really nice sports cars. I bragged and showed my car off to everyone I worked with. We created web pages dedicated to our cars, jammed with photos of mods (modifications) and wish lists for future projects. We both joined car clubs. It was awesome. We were living the high life, and money was flying out of our pockets as fast as we were hitting the gas pedal. Eventually though, the high of that first year began to wear off. I got tired of always parking in the back of every parking lot I drove into. It always seemed to rain the day after I washed the car. The gas and insurance bills were a constant drag, while my free company car had neither, as my employer covered those costs. Out of nowhere my friend got laid off from his job. He was suddenly forced to live on unemployment, and could no longer afford his car. He fell behind in the payments. The car had depreciated faster than the outstanding balance of his loan had, and he was also unable to sell. One morning while he was sleeping, his awesome Mustang was repossessed. My car, on the other hand was driven less and less, until eventually I sold it through classifieds to a private buyer. The new buyer luckily paid about three thousand more than what I owed (due to the aftermarket parts), but if you really focused on all of the money I invested (which was in excess of $10,000 in parts and stereo equipment, plus another $15,000 in payments, maintenance, and gas), I truly lost a lot of money.

• **Takeaway** – Each of us made the huge mistake wasting time financing depreciating assets, when we could have been paying off debt and investing. We both missed a huge opportunity to live debt free. The worst part though, was that my buddy, who had his car repossessed, continued to have to pay off the remaining balance more than five years after it was repossessed.

Conclusion

Are you excited to start applying debt management techniques and concepts to your personal finances? Well I hope so, because you need momentum! Assess your debts and apply the Debt Snowball. Focus on the 50/50 Rule. Where are you? If you find yourself paying out around 70% - 80% or more of your take home salary to bills or debts, then you are 20% - 30% overextended. Are you house poor, where the vast majority of your take home pay goes into your home? Maybe it is time to consider downsizing. The same concept applies to new car buyers. Investing large amounts of your net income into depreciating assets is a guaranteed way to never get ahead. Build your own budget charts and balance sheets. Add savings categories even if you have a zero balance. Sign up for sites or apps like Mint.com, and begin tracking your cash, credit cards, loans, investments, and property. Wipe away the fog and see through your windshield for the first time. Make a change; do it today; do it for good; do it for your family; and do it for yourself.

<u>Money Tips</u>

• Build your own budget. Add each bill, due date, frequency, and whether the bill is on auto-pay or not.

• Calculate your percentage of net income to net bills. Where are your finances at when applying the 50/50 Rule? If you pay over 50%, you are overextended.

• Manage your debts by building a Debt Snowball chart. Include each debt name, balance and interest rate. Filter in tax implications if possible.

• Create a balance sheet to track your assets, liabilities, and net worth.

• Research finance websites and create a finance folder in your browser.

• Download debt management apps such as Mint, to assist you.

INCOME

It is very important to understand that there are three different types of income: Earned Income, Unearned Income, and Portfolio Income. Knowing the difference between each type, as well as knowing the meaning of each, can greatly affect your finances and can be essential to your financial future. The differences are vast and need to be considered in order for you to map out the potholes. Moving forward, consider the following:

Figure 1.

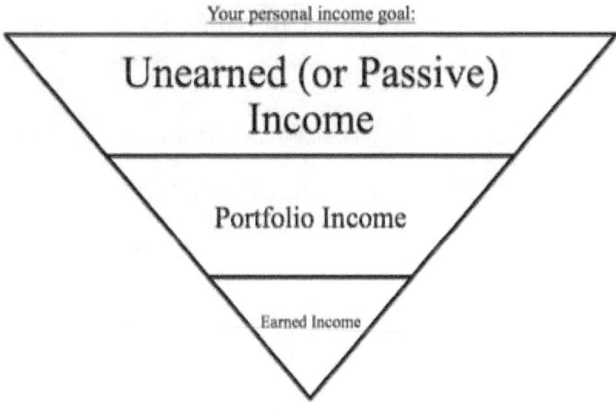

Earned (or Active) Income

The first type of income is referred to as earned (or ordinary) income. Per IRS.gov, earned income is defined as "all the taxable income and wages you get from working or from certain disability payments. There are two types of earned income: You work for someone who pays you or you own or run a business or farm." [15] Important takeaways, which you need to know about earned income, are:

• Earned income is made by actively working – Whether it be for an employer or on your own, going into the office from nine to five, or opening shop as a small business owner, earned income is what you make for actively working.

• Earned income is the highest taxed type of income – The greatest percentage of our population makes earned income, rather than unearned or portfolio income. The government focuses their efforts on taxing earned income because it is easily accessible, as well as the largest cumulative revenue stream. Think of a bear watching a school of salmon swimming up the river.

• The number one selling feature of American culture is the concept of "The American Dream;" that anyone can to go to school, obtain a great career, buy a home, and start a family. It's the sexy red dress or fancy new sports car that we all strive to obtain. It has the ability to make us better than which we currently are. In truth, The American Dream has never been the statistical norm, but rather the standard obtained by those in the upper-middle to lower-upper class. We're motivated to achieve it because the concept has the ability to make us feel below average.

• A pension is considered earned income, as it is a benefit or payments made to you, due to actively working.

Unearned (or Passive) Income

What is the opposite of earned income? The answer is unearned income, or money that you make without working. Per Wikipedia.org (2014, para. 2), "The American Internal Revenue Service defines passive income as only coming from two sources: rental activity or trade or business activities in which you do not materially participate." [16] Unearned income is what is never brought up, explained or instructed on how to obtain it. It's the dirty little secret nobody wants you to know about, because once you jump out of the earned income stream, you're one less fish to gulp. There are also great tax benefits to unearned income, which we will cover later in our chapter on taxes. Think of unearned income as a shortcut on your journey to the land of wealth. If you could take a short cut, would you? Why take the long road when a new highway could take you there in half the time? The following are examples of unearned income:

• Peer-2-peer lending – Brought about due to a market need stemming from an unwillingness of traditional banks to offer personal loan products, peer-2-peer lending fills a void, and offers a solution for people who would not otherwise qualify for a personal loan due to poor credit. It also fills the void for those looking for debt consolidation with a lower rate, or those who are looking to make home improvements. The way it works is that John Doe will post that he needs $10,000 because he wants to renovate his kitchen. Since John cannot get a bank loan due to his 525 credit score, or he just doesn't want to deal with the banks, this is an easy source to secure the cash he is looking for. Eventually, one or more people who have assessed John as a risk (this can be anyone looking to lend money as an investment, and make interest) and feel that he was worth the investment on their part will fill the order for $10,000. When John repays his loan, those who lent him money are now essentially the bank; however, working through the website medium. Each lender will recover their principal investment plus interest through John's repayments. The only risk they run is whether John was worth investing in. If John defaults or files for bankruptcy, then the peer-2-peer lender will not recover their investment. The secret to peer-2-peer lending is if you are lending money, the more loans you lend to, the lower your risk. As with all investments, you must diversify.

• Rental Property – There are numerous success stories regarding people who invest in rental properties due to their steady stream of returning unearned income for years to come.

Sure there are going to be some headaches along the way, caused by bad tenants, property maintenance, and lackluster management companies; however, at some point the property will be paid off, and at that point, the profits will far exceed the expenses. The more renters a landlord can squeeze into a property, the more profitable they may be. For example, a duplex has the potential to make more profit than a single family home, just as an apartment complex would make more income than a triplex. The more rentals within one property, the better.

• Land – Just by owning the right piece of land, you have the potential to generate a lifetime of unearned income. Mineral rights to land could potentially generate revenue in the form of oil or natural gas. A phone company may want to place a cellular tower on the property, which they will then pay you to rent the land. A utility company may place wind turbines on the property to generate electricity. If the property is along a highway, billboards can be installed with residual advertising revenue. A developer could also approach you about developing the land, and pay millions. Seriously consider investing in strategic pieces of land if the opportunity presents itself.

Portfolio Income

The last type of income is Portfolio income. Per Investopdia.com (2014, para. 1), the definition of portfolio income is: "Income from investments, dividends, interest, royalties and capital gains.

Portfolio income does not come from passive investments and is not earned through normal business activity." [17] The following are examples of portfolio income:

• Stocks/Bonds/Funds – Publically traded stocks, bonds and mutual funds have the ability to generate portfolio income in the form of dividends and capital gains.

• Commodities – Per investopedia.com (2014, para. 2-4), a commodity is:

> "Any good exchanged during commerce, which includes goods traded on a commodity exchange. The sale and purchase of commodities is usually carried out through futures contracts on exchanges that standardize the quantity and minimum quality of the commodity being traded. For example, the Chicago Board of Trade stipulates that one wheat contract is for 5,000 bushels and also states what grades of wheat (e.g. No. 2 Northern Spring) can be used to satisfy the contract." [18]

Additional examples of commodities are things like coffee, copper, corn, cotton, oats, rice, sugar, etc. Keep in mind that in order to invest in commodities, that you must be able to show that your net worth meets a specific threshold.

• Certificate of Deposit (CD) – A certificate of deposit (CD) is a time deposit, commonly sold in the United States by banks, thrift institutions, and credit unions. [19] The benefit to a CD is that it is insured over a fixed period of time, or in other words, guaranteed money. The downside is that the return on CDs is typically low, because they are guaranteed. Therefore CDs are always set to very low rates of interest.

• Royalties – books, EBooks, music or anything else with a copyright has the potential of generating royalties to you for doing nothing. Each time a book is sold, a piece of music is played, or a patented technology is utilized, it will generate income to you without effort. A great example of royalties is the story of Michael Jackson owning the Beatles music catalogue. The catalogue alone is worth millions due to the daily radio airplays of Beatles songs across the globe. Many former record executives own royalties, which eventually get passed down to their heirs.

Our Story – Living Paycheck-to-Paycheck on Earned Income Only Pothole

• **Situation** – Wake up. Go to work. Come home. Go to bed. Repeat. Wait for payday. Pay bills. Spend check immediately. Countdown for two weeks until next payday. We were trapped in the rat race. All of our money was being spent within the first three days following payday. We were never going to get ahead. The biggest problem, though, was the one that we didn't even know we had: all of our income was coming from earned (or active) income generated from working for an employer. We had no outside income or alternative investments. We were living one life event away from being in big trouble.

• **Task** – Get out of the paycheck-to-paycheck pothole.

• **Action** – Our first action toward investing in unearned and portfolio income was paying down our current debt. There is no point in investing when the thousands of dollars in interest are offsetting the interest you are making. We agreed to pay off debt and invest in the alternative income streams. We incorporated the debt snowball as well as set goals for incorporating alternative streams of income.

• **Result** – Today we are well on our way to earning alternative income. Our debt is dropping significantly each month, while we plan out new web-based businesses. The glory of a web-based business is that it is not like a physical business where you need to be present seven days a week, all day long. There are plenty of ways to make money from the web, while doing nothing. We also are planning to get into peer-2-peer lending – as a lender. Outside of my day job, I started writing this book for example, that hopefully will generate income at some point down the road. I've also written screenplays, which I hope to convert into eBooks, along with a kid's book. Any money generated will be considered unearned income. The icing on the cake will be our first rental property.

• **Takeaway** – We've had years to invest in alternative streams of income, yet we never did for the main reason that we wasted our money on depreciating assets that didn't matter. We also didn't fully understand or know the concepts of unearned and portfolio income, therefore we really didn't even know they existed. The lesson learned was to stop investing in depreciating assets and start investing in alternative streams of income.

Conclusion

It is important that you understand different types of income so that you know where you need to focus your efforts on getting ahead in the long run. A financial foundation is built upon compounding decisions, and how all of your choices (large and small) can add up. Focus on the type of income and invest in alternative income streams. Also remember, that prior to any investment, you need to erase your debts. Even if you are able to invest in alternative income while still holding a debt balance, the money going out to pay interest will offset the money coming in. make sure the interest payments are only going one way – into your wallet.

Money Tips

• Start your own list of alternative income streams that appeal to you in your situation. Explore the possibility of adding a few others, which you previously have not considered.

• Research and locate an investment or rental property.

• Consider investing in peer-2-peer lending. Look to websites such as lendingclub.com or prosper.com. You could also consider becoming an angel investor.

• Make it your goal to move away from earned or active income as your main source of support. Diversify your income to alleviate risk.

INVESTING

Once you've reached your goal to live overhead free it is time to start thinking about investment. There are a lot of investment options out there. Which one is the best for you, depends on what your goal is. It is also important to recognize that there is a lot more to investing than mindlessly having a portion of your salary auto-deducted into a 401(k) account. Ahead, we are going to look into different investment options, and the best ways to accomplish your goals while avoiding potholes. We will narrow our focus on investment by dividing it into three categories: self-investment, unearned investment, and portfolio investment.

Self-Investment

Self-investment is the first type of investment option. Self-investment may or may not be the most advantageous investment option; however, it is most likely the most common, due to the egocentric aspect of it. Navigating self-investment potholes can be quite a challenge, as there are so many ways for your personal finance vehicle to get caught in a bad situation. Lets first explore and dissect self-investment options, which may or may not be available to you.

Primary Residence

Owning your own home is a goal that is pushed and engrained into our lives from childhood through adulthood. It can be a great investment, if you know what you are looking for and what you are doing. What is your property goal? When I look at property, I like to specifically focus on resale, because I've lived through the not-so-fun experience of losing a lot of money in a home sale. In a primary residence the following factors can greatly influence your investment and should be considered anytime you are seriously considering buying a new property.

• Location – The most important factor in home investment. Are you purchasing in an area that is highly desirable or are you looking at a fringe area that has a great price? What you need to know is that the lower price is going to come at a cost. There are numerous implications that a not-so-desirable location can have on any future re-sale, thus it is important that if you are choosing a fringe area, it has a few things going for it, such as demographic, amenities, and schools.

• Neighborhood Demographic – What are the demographics of the neighborhood, of which you are looking? Are you a young family looking for a neighborhood with lots of kids? If so, you may not want to consider a neighborhood with retirees. Young families also have different amenity needs versus older families or retirees. Typically the neighborhoods with lots of young families are also going to be in the areas with the best school districts.

• Neighborhood Amenities – Does the neighborhood offer a swimming pool or tennis court for residents? Maybe the neighborhood offers nature trails or biking. A lot of newer neighborhoods offer elaborate splash parks, full of water slides and lagoon pools, to entice as many buyers as possible. They may offer a gym for the adults, and playgrounds for the kids. Athletic fields and lap pools are marketed to the young adults. What amenities does the neighborhood offer? If the answer does not line up with your family goals, as well as resale goals, a strong argument can be made for looking elsewhere.

• School district – One of the most important factors in home investment. You could own the greatest home in the city, with the best renovations; however, if your assigned school district is below average, your home will not generate the resale interest it deserves. With the advent of real estate websites and apps such as

Zillow.com, Trulia.com, and Realtor.com, it is very easy to get a bird's eye view of which geographic areas have the best school districts. I know when we were looking for a home I didn't even consider areas with below average school districts, and only focused on those with stellar reputations. Nobody wants their kids to get a below average education, so school district should be your number one factor when buying a home, whether you have your own kids or not.

• Age of the home – The age of a home can make a big difference to which buyers your home may appeal. There is common stereotype that an older home is going to require renovations while a new home may not. Part of this is true, due to changes in the building code (especially in regards to roofing, electrical, and plumbing); however, I would not agree with the statement that new homes don't require maintenance. Depending on the builder, a new home may have just as many problems, if not more than an established home, due to spotty and poor workmanship. In our current home, we've had multiple plumbing-related water losses due to a poor job by the plumbers on our home. If you are looking at an older or historic home it is very important that the roof, electrical, and plumbing have all been upgraded to code, as well as any additions or alterations have the proper permits and documentation. It is also important that any recalled items have been replaced and there is documentation to prove it.

• Kitchen and Bathrooms – Behind location and school district, the single other largest selling factor within a home is the quality of the kitchen and bathrooms. The kitchen and bathrooms can make or break a house as well as any sale. People often times overlook external factors because they're blinded by a fancy kitchen or matching bathrooms. High-end finishes, and building materials such as granite, marble, slate, hardwood floors, etc. are desired by the vast majority of homebuyers. Make sure your home has as many high-end materials installed as possible prior to you moving in, as renovations can be costly depending on the project. Throw on top of fancy materials; an excellent staging job, and just about any home will sell.

• Fees and Home Owner's Association (HOA) Dues – Also very important in your investment as well as in your marketing to a future buyer is the additional cost of any community development district (CDD) fees, Home Owner's Association (HOA) fees, as well any additional special assessments currently in place against the residents of the community. We once looked at a great condo, with vaulted ceilings, wood flooring throughout, 2000sq. ft. and a ton of potential. We ultimately however, passed on making an offer, when we discovered that the condo association fees alone were over $600 a month. Big fees can make, break, or continuously block your sale.

• Neighbors – Look around the home at the immediate neighbors. Are there lawns that haven't been mowed in weeks or damaged or broken down cars in the driveway? What about sex offenders? Is there a sexual predator in the neighborhood? How about standard renters, vacation renter, or group homes? Are there a lot of homes rented to college kids in the neighborhood? Weigh the quality of the neighbors prior to any investment. Don't get me wrong, as there are always a lot of great neighbors even in a neighborhood with a few questionable ones; however, you have to consider red flags and the potential impact on your investment.

• Nearby Foreclosures – What is the percentage of foreclosure homes within a half-mile, mile, or five-mile radius of the property you are looking at? In today's real estate market, foreclosures are common, and not just in the lower income neighborhoods, but equally common within the high-income neighborhoods. Remember that each foreclosure has the potential to drive down the potential sale and harm your investment, thus it's important to get a clear picture of the volume of foreclosures in the immediate surrounding area.

Personal Auto(s)

Unless you are living in a downtown urban area such as New York, Washington D.C., Chicago, or Boston, you're most likely going to need a car at some point. Though all vehicles should be considered a depreciating asset, it is important to consider them as an investment as well. Investing in the right vehicle can set you up for years of success, while investing in the wrong one can leave you with years of car payments (debts). Parameters for auto investing include but are not limited to the following:

• Five years old – This should become your new standard for purchasing a car. No longer will you be driving a new car off the lot due to how fast the depreciation applies. Let someone else cover that initial cost for you.

• No more financing – buy your vehicles in cash and save yourself years of interest payments.

• Private sellers only – Buying from a private seller will not only save you from the uncomfortable trip of going to a car dealer and haggling over a price, but it will also save you from all of the additional dealer fees, maintenance plans, and additional costs. My experience with buying a car from a dealership versus a private seller, is that the additional cost can be anywhere from $1,500 to $2,000 or more, for the exact same vehicle. With the

Internet, you should be able to look up a car's value at Kelley Blue Book (KBB.com), as well its history in a CARFAX Report, based upon the vehicle identification number (VIN). Try looking at AutoTrader.com, and filter down exactly to what you are looking for, which presents the greatest opportunity for a good deal.

• Focus on efficiency – Whether it is miles per gallon (mpg), electric versus gasoline, car versus truck, or storage space versus compact, focus on the most efficient vehicle for you. Can you apply the purchase of this vehicle to a personal business?

• Remember the purpose of your investment – The purpose of buying a vehicle is to get you from point A to point B, without burdening you with years of car payments. If your secondary purpose is to get a sports car, fancy truck, tricked-out jeep or some other vehicle, remember to stick to your principles first, and your wants second. If you have the extra money and enjoy working on cars as a hobby, find the best deal and invest. The only warning I would issue here is that once you start investing in a vehicle, it may be quite challenging to stop.

Personal Business

Investing in a personal business can be a rewarding, life-changing event. Most personal business owners will attest that "it is what you make of it." That being said, a lot of personal businesses don't make any money for the first couple of years, and lots of personal businesses fail. There can be quite a lot of risk depending on what type of personal business you are attempting to open, what your experience level is in the industry, and how detailed your business plan is. It is essential that you have a clearly defined set of expectations to manage your investment. Without a business plan, you may as well be throwing out bricks of cash in the air on a windy day. Make sure you navigate personal business ownership by having a plan.

The most common type of personal business is typically a limited liability corporation (LLC). The reason so many start LLC's is because the corporation acts as a buffer around the business owner's personal assets. In other words, if things ever go south within the business, the owner can rest easy that they will not have their personal assets confiscated when someone sues them. It is also very easy to start an LLC and anyone can do it. File the proper forms within your state, either directly through the state resources, your bank, or have a third party do it for you. Examples of third parties that will file your business for you are: LegalZoom.com or RocketLawyer.com. Both sites will file all of the appropriate forms and manage the liability of your LLC, for an up-charged price around $300 - $600.

Once your LLC is formed you may want or need to invest in a website. You can secure a domain name through a multitude of sites from GoDaddy.com to NameCheap.com. After securing the domain, the next step is to have your site built. I recommend SiteBuilderReport.com, if you're not sure whom to go with. The website is great because it clearly dissects the pros and cons of the various website builders, in order to give you a better understanding of which company may work best for you. If you're looking to go big time with a completely custom website, check out the web design rankings on TopSEOs.com. Here is where you find the big players for custom websites. Keep in mind however, that the disclaimer for pursuing one of the TopSEOs companies is that the price to build could run you anywhere from $25,000 and up.

For start-up capital, I recommend spending your own money and shying away from financing. Going back to our principle that any loan or credit is a form of overextending yourself, I would not recommend taking out a small business loan, as you are again assuming that not only will the business you are starting be profitable, but that you will also have continuous revenue to repay the loan. If you don't have the revenue, you're probably going to go bankrupt. You are also assuming that a significant life event will not intervene anywhere in the process, which is something that you can never assume. The biggest advantage to funding your small business on your own is that if it does become successful, you can assume all of the profit without debt. Always be thinking about the little pie slices; do you really want to give away part of your hard-earned pie to loan interest and creditors? I didn't think so.

Kid's college fund

If you are a parent, investing in your child's college education is extremely important to set your child up to not only be college educated, but to graduate without being saddled with a life of debt repayment. I like to think of saving for my son's college like a backup plan to him landing a scholarship. The main goal of your child should always be to get a scholarship first. If a scholarship is unavailable to them, the military is an option due to the GI bill. For the sake of investment, we are going to talk about 529 plans (or prepaid savings plans, which you can invest in).

What is a 529 plan? "A 529 plan is a tax-advantaged investment vehicle in the United States designed to encourage saving for the future higher education expenses of a designed beneficiary. 529 plans are named after section 529 of the Internal Revenue Code 26 U.S.C. § 529. [20] Per the College Savings Plans Network, (2010, para. 3):

> While most plans allow investors from out of state, there can be significant state tax advantages and other benefits, such as matching grant and scholarship opportunities, protection from creditors and exemption from state financial aid calculations for investors who invest in 529 plans in their state of residence." [21]

529 plans can be broken down into two categories: prepaid plans and savings plans. Per Wikipedia (2014, para. 4-5): "Prepaid plans may be administered by states or higher education institutions," and "allow one to purchase tuition credits at today's rates to be used in the future. Performance is based upon tuition inflation." [20] Locking up a prepaid plan at today's rates could be very beneficial for your child with the rising costs of higher education. For example, if the cost of education continues to rise, your plan will be based upon tuition hours, rather than cost, thus your money is going to go a lot further than someone without a plan.

Additional parameters of 529 plans which you should be aware of are:

- Savings plans are different in that all growth is based upon market performance of the underlying investments, which typically consist of mutual funds.

- Most 529 savings plans offer a variety of age-based asset allocation options where the underlying investments become more conservative as the beneficiary gets closer to college age.

- Although states administer savings plans, record-keeping and administrative service for many savings plans is usually delegated to a mutual fund company or other financial services company. [20]

So in other words, just as you would invest in mutual funds within your retirement account, if you choose to invest in a 529 plan your plan is going to perform in line with your investment choices.

Re-education

Are you thinking of going back to school to secure a higher-paying job? What about starting a new career in a completely different field? It is never too late to go back to school. For those who are already in the workforce, going back to school can be very challenging due to scheduling conflicts, home life/family balance, and cost. My personal experience from taking graduate level courses was that the cost was nearly triple that of undergraduate courses. It was also quite challenging to be able to meet the time commitment required to enroll, study, and pass courses. Regardless of the obstacles, if you are committed, advancing your education is always a good thing. Please see the following list of ways to pay for a graduate degree without racking up new student loans (which should be avoided at all costs):

1. Employer Reimbursement – Your employer may offer college tuition reimbursement. Parameters are going to be in place; however, limiting the employers' contribution, contingent on your length of employment, whether you are a full-time employee or not, the degree path chosen, and the final grades earned. Employer reimbursement plans may stipulate that upon graduation you must work for the employer for an extended amount of years (possibly between 3-5) prior to leaving the company. Regardless of the stipulation, employee reimbursement plans accomplish your goals twofold: they pay for your graduate degree, while saving you from a mountain of debt.

2. Graduate Assistant/Adjunct Professor – By working for the college or university you are attending, you may be able to land a free ride, where the school will cover the full costs of your graduate degree in exchange for your teaching services. This is a

win-win scenario for you and the school, as you can secure your degree, while the school can obtain your discounted services.

3. Savings – Stock-piling your money for school should be looked at as more of a last ditch option, due to the amount of money you would need to save. Keep in mind that if you can only save for one class at a time, then that's all you can do, and that is okay. The problem though, is by saving for college yourself; the time delay can potentially stagnate your progress and derail you from your goals. Going with the savings option takes time and dedication. My personal thoughts are that you would be better off with employer reimbursement.

4. Join the military – Enlist or sign up for the reserve in order to secure the GI bill. However, in order to be eligible for the GI bill, you must meet the following requirements per the U.S. Department of Veterans Affairs (2014, para. 5-8):

> • Have a six-year obligation to serve in the Selected Reserve signed after June 30, 1985. If you are an officer, you must have agreed to serve six years in addition to your original obligation. For some types of training, it is necessary to have a six-year commitment that begins after Sept. 30, 1990.
>
> • Complete your initial active duty for training (IADT).
>
> • Meet the requirement to receive a high school diploma or equivalency certificate before completing IADT. You

may not use twelve hours toward a college degree to meet this requirement.

• Remain in good standing while serving in an active Selected Reserve unit. You will also retain MGIB-SR eligibility if you were discharged from Selected Reserve service due to a disability that was not caused by misconduct. Your eligibility period may be extended if you are ordered to active duty. [22]

Retirement

When is the best time to invest in a retirement account? The answer is the sooner the better. Due to the concept of compound interest (interest which adds to the principal), the longer your money is in the account, the more interest it will generate. Thus, the earlier you start investing, the higher the potential return can be. What you need to be aware of are the potholes in retirement investing (fees and taxes) for either violating retirement account rules, as well as the costs of investing with an advisor. It is up to you to choose which retirement options are going to be best for you. I suggest you go with multiple options.

• Pension – Securing a pension should be your retirement goal number one. The catch, though, is that not all employers offer pensions, thus you have to be choosy with your employer's benefit package. The way a pension typically works is that you have to work for the employer for a specified amount of time in order to become vested. Once vested, whether you continue working for that particular employer or not, you are entitled to a percentage of the pension, based upon your time worked for the employer. At age sixty-five, the pension will begin to pay out based on your years of service with company, stability of the pension, employer, state, etc. A word of caution should be mentioned here in regards to government-related pensions, as they are often easy targets for political talking points. Depending on whoever is in office (especially in state and local governments), may ultimately determine the stability of your pension.

• 401(k) – One of the most common retirement options is the 401(k) account. The way a 401(k) account works is that an employer will typically match up to 100% of 3%-8% of your salary, if you choose to invest in it. Therefore, if your employer were offering a 100% match at 5%, if your salary was $40,000 a year and you invested $2,000, your employer would also contribute $2,000, totaling $4,000 in your account at the end of the year. If based on your yearly allocations (bonds, mutual funds, and stocks), your account earned a 5% return in compound interest (or $45.43), at the end of the year you would have $4045.43 Some employers even offer more than 4%, up to 8% (though this is rare). If you choose not to invest in your 401(k), you are essentially leaving benefits (free, untaxed money) on the table. The downside of a 401(k) is that you are contributing under the assumption that you will live to fifty-nine and one half years old, which may not happen. If you choose to take a withdrawal before fifty-nine and a half, you can plan on paying a 10% early withdrawal penalty, plus income tax. You may also have the option to take a loan out against your 401(k) without the penalties. Though the money loaned may seem great at first, you're ultimately going to pay the price in your paycheck, as repayments will be deducted until the loan balance is paid. Ultimately, my view is that you should never leave tax-free money, which is owed to you on the table. However, if you are going to contribute to a 401(k), you should be overhead and debt free prior to investment.

• Individual Retirement Account (IRA) – A retirement account offered by financial institutions that provides tax advantages. The following are the most common types of IRAs:

    o Traditional IRA – Tax-deductible contributions from pre-tax assets (money). All transactions and earnings within the IRA have no tax impact, while withdrawals at retirement are taxed as income.

o Roth IRA – Contributions are made with after-tax assets. All transactions within the IRA have no tax impact, while withdrawals are tax-free.

o SEP IRA – A provision that allows an employer (typically a small business or self-employed individual) to make retirement plan contributions into a Traditional IRA established in the employee's name, instead of to a pension fund in the company's name.

o SIMPLE IRA – A Savings Incentive Match Plan for Employees that requires employer-matching contributions to the plan whenever an employee makes a contribution. Similar to a 401(k) plan, but with lower contribution limits and simpler (less costly) administration. Although termed an IRA, it is treated separately. [23]

• Annuities (a non-taxable investment) – As described by *CNN Money*, "an annuity is an insurance product that pays out income, and can be used as part of a retirement strategy." Annuities are a popular choice for older adults who may be contributing to their retirement account later in life because annuities do not have a yearly contribution limit. Annuities are also a "popular choice for investors who want to receive a steady income stream in retirement. The income you receive from an annuity can be doled out monthly, quarterly, annually or even in a lump sum payment," which is "determined by a variety of factors, including the length of your payment period. You can opt to receive payments for the rest of your life, or for a set number of years. How much you receive depends on whether you opt for a guaranteed payout (fixed annuity) or a payout stream determined by the performance of your annuity's underlying investments (variable annuity)." The disadvantage with annuities comes in the form of the fees charged for them. "Financial planners and insurance salesmen will frequently try to steer seniors or other people in various stages toward retirement into annuities." Commissions can be "as much as 10% or so," while taking money out of an annuity after just a few years after investing can result in a surrender charge that "typically runs about 7% of your account value," and "up to 20% in the first year." It is not uncommon for an additional "2% to 3% a year" to be tacked on various annual fees. "Also, as with a 401(k) or IRA, in an annuity it's generally not a good idea to take out any money until you reach age 59 ½ because withdrawals made prior to that are hit with a 10% early withdrawal penalty." [24]

Ultimately, the best option for investing in your retirement is investing in living your life overhead free, because if you think it is challenging paying all of your bills now, just try doing it on a fixed income like social security.

<u>Savings/Emergency Fund</u>

Investing in an emergency fund needs to be one of your priorities, if you are planning to wean yourself off of credit. I recommend having one account with at least $1,000, in it, if not more. You should have enough to cover incidentals, such as replacement of an appliance, or an unexpected doctor bill. Many experts recommend you have at least three months of savings, in case you were to lose your job; however, for most people, saving up for three months of living is just not possible. If you have the extra money, save the additional; if not, just focus on the $1,000. If you want to get ahead of debt and leave credit cards behind forever, an emergency fund is a must.

You should invest in a savings account if you are actively trying to save toward a goal. For example, saving up for a down payment on a property, buying a vehicle, going on vacation, or preparing for taxes, saving for a purpose makes sense, and is a worthwhile investment. Saving, just to have savings, doesn't make sense, due to the rate of inflation. You would be better off putting the money into an alternative investment, where you will be able to make a higher rate of return, as most savings accounts offer interest rates, which are typically less than inflation. Save for a purpose, otherwise you may be losing money.

Unearned (Passive) Investment

The next category of investments is unearned (or passive) investments, or the investments, which give you income for doing nothing other than investing. We've already covered some of these topics in earlier chapters, so now we will just focus on the investment side.

Peer-2-Peer Lending

For the borrower, peer-2-peer lending offers an easily accessible way to obtain funds to consolidate debt or start a renovation, while avoiding more standard lending institutions such as the local bank. For the lender, what peer-2-peer lending gives you, is the option to choose the risk (person requesting a loan), measure the risk, and decide whether to invest your money in their request or not. You may be the only person lending, or one of many, depending on the amount of the request. One example is LendingClub.com, which offers the ability for you to automatically invest based on your defined criteria. In order to automatically invest, however, an investor must show a:

"Minimum required account value to participate: $2,500."

Lending Club also measures and provides historical returns by grade (A Grade = 4.77%, B Grade = 7.05%, C

Grade = 8.24%, D Grade = 18.17%, E Grade = 20.96%, F Grade = 23.23%, G Grade = 24.41%). (Lending Club, Copyright 2006-2014. All Rights Reserved). [25]

The important thing to remember is that the interest rate is directly correlated with the risk, thus the riskier the loan, the higher the potential return. On the downside, there is always a chance that the borrower could default and wipe out your investment, and with the higher risk, the greater the chance of default.

The bottom line is that investing in peer-2-peer lending is worth the risk as long as you diversify your investment. Based on the statistics on LendingClub.com, the returns offered far exceed the interest of a standard savings account.

Certificate of Deposit

From an investment perspective, certificates of deposit (CDs) are one of the easiest portfolio investment options. The advantages of CDs are that the money invested has a guaranteed rate of return, meaning your investment will materialize to you at a guaranteed point in time. There is no guesswork or continual maintenance when it comes to a CD, making it easy money. Unfortunately, with such a low maintenance investment, comes a price. The downside to CDs is that, because they are guaranteed, they typically offer low rates. The shorter the CD period, the lower the rate, and the longer the CD period, the higher the rate. With a quick check of Bankrate.com you can see that you would be lucky to invest in a CD with a rate in excess of 2%. With a CD being a locked investment, they also lose their liquidity, meaning you cannot just pull your money out of them whenever you would like. Some investors like to set up a CD ladder. The way the ladder works is that they always invest in the longest time period (typically five years), but follow each investment with an additional investment every three to six months. Eventually, after five years, their first investment will mature, followed by the next and so on, and they will continue to reinvest. My personal view is that due to the low rate of return, illiquidity and extended investment, CDs are a great option for anyone who is already wealthy and looking for a low maintenance place to make money.

Property

Making an investment in property is one the best things you can do to increase your future income. Investing in property has made lots of people wealthy, whether by a quick flip or by steady long-term unearned rental income. Those who own property often acquire additional properties as well, by either taking out lines of credit on their existing portfolio, or by re-investing their rental income. It is not uncommon for a steady real estate investor to go from one property to two, three, and so on. A property snowball is a real possibility and something that you can do.

It is also very important that you understand the potential potholes with real estate; due to the substantial cash investment it is going to require securing your portfolio. For example, if you purchase a newly renovated property that was much higher in price than the comparative properties in the neighborhood, you may have completely wiped out your opportunity for equity. Always check the comparatives. On the other hand, if you miscalculate, and choose a property with substantial unseen issues, you may be stuck with a lemon that could steadily suck your wallet dry with all of the unforeseen repairs and liens.

In order to properly invest, you first must come up with a plan to avoid potholes by creating a goal and formulating a framework or parameters to achieve that goal.

• Flipping (considered a short-term high-risk investment) – begins with locating a distressed property within your local area. A good potential flip should stand out if the comparative sales of homes in the neighborhood are significantly higher than the property you have chosen. Check the property records as well to research the purchase prices of past homeowners. Assess the neighborhood, schools, and street noise. Assess the type of property listing, whether it is a private, short sale, foreclosure, or bank-owned property. If you are planning a flip, it is also best to check the property out beforehand with your contractor to assess the rehab and place an additional dollar figure for it. Once the determination is made to purchase the property, a cash offer will be required to secure the sale. A strict timetable or schedule should be followed if possible because the sooner the property is ready, the sooner you make your money. After rehabbing the bones, professional staging should be considered to make sure your property looks its best. Think of it like applying for a job: you wear a suit and tie versus gym shorts and sandals. List the property for the max based on the comparative sales and hope for the best. Never get emotionally attached to a property and always stick to your parameters.

- Rental property (considered a long-term low-risk investment) – starts with either finding a distressed property or one that is going to be your short-term principal residence (1-2 years). A good rental property is going to be in a kid-friendly area, with a good school district, or somewhere like a college town that easily sustains long-term rentals. Middle-class urban areas are also good to look at; however, remember that location is everything. Make sure that you purchase in an area where you can not only secure renters, but also sell the property if you need to. Don't buy a rental property in the middle of nowhere just because it has a good price. A strong indicator of cash flow is a property that will hold more than one renter (i.e. duplex, triplex, quad, etc.). Make sure that if you are going to finance a rental property that you save at least 20% (if not more) of the total sales price to put toward the loan. Anything less than 20% and you can forget financing, in which case you better have the money for an all-cash offer. Once you have secured the property, compare other rentals in the local market to see if your price is in line. Lastly, mitigate any further risk by allocating additional funds for emergency repairs, upgrades, and insurance.

- Investment property/land – Buying a parcel of land can be a great investment if it is in the right location. Purchasing land that is in a location that is on the verge of being developed is one option. Buy up pieces of land in a popular area and upsell them at a profit. Another option is to look for parcels that have the potential for natural resource profits, such as oil, natural gas, etc. As we've already discussed, leasing a high wind area to the local utilities to set up windmills could also generate significant income. Allowing a cellular carrier to set up a tower could also generate income (though I understand this probably isn't very common). Land along highways or popular roads can also be used for billboards and advertising revenues. Start thinking of uses for land and how you can make money off of it.

<u>Royalties</u>

Investing in royalty streams of income depends on which royalty producing option you are going to go with. Below are examples of things you can do to generate royalties.

• Patent Technology, Inventions or Ideas – A lot of inventors who nobody has ever heard of are loaded (or filthy rich) because they patented a piece of technology or idea at some point in time that someone else needed permission to us and paid a royalty. What also happens is that often ideas are stolen. The person who invented the technology will typically bring a lawsuit, which will either be settled pre-trial or post. Eventually the party who patented the technology almost always gets paid. In Silicon Valley (where some of the largest software companies in the world are located), there are often patent battles between competing software companies such as Google, Apple, Yahoo, etc. The large companies try to gobble up as many patents as possible, just so they can win lawsuits. There are even numerous shell corporations that do nothing but hold patents for just such a reason. They are also rich.

• Become an author – Put pen to paper or fingers to keys and start writing. Write books, EBooks, movie scripts, poems, etc. Each sale will generate income into your pocket.

• Write music – Becoming a musician and writing original compositions can be very lucrative. Whether it is commercial jingles, songs for other people, or songs for themselves or their band, many musicians become very wealthy due to airplay. Each time a song is played on the air; revenue is generated, which is later paid at the end of the month. Think of all of the popular artists who are constant rotation on the radio stations where you live. Just one hit song, could make you rich for the rest of your life.

• Purchase pre-existing royalty producing investments – An example is Michael Jackson purchasing the Beatles catalogue. Owning the rights to one popular song could generate instant revenue indefinitely. The catch with purchasing music rights is that unless you're connected within the record industry (to a former A/R executive), accomplishing this might be quite challenging.

Portfolio Investment

Our last set of investments is portfolio investments, which typically consist of stocks, bonds, mutual funds, and commodities. The benefit to having a portfolio investment versus any other is that your investment is only a real-time sale away from becoming liquid. In other words, you can usually sell a portfolio investment in real time and get cash back, which is great if you need money in a pinch. Another benefit to portfolio investments is that they are easily accessible to anyone looking to invest. The catch though, is that with easy accessibility there are various sharks waiting to prey on you (the novice investor) and take your investment. It is very important that you are aware of your surroundings when making a portfolio investment.

Stocks

In order to be successful in the stock market, you need to research and follow the teachings of successful investors. "Be fearful when others are greedy, and greedy when others are fearful," [26] is a piece of advice offered by Warren Buffett. I love Buffett's quote, as it cuts straight to the heart of all of the misinformation that comes out of Wall Street. Think of all of the self-proclaimed stock experts who highlight each an every high and low on a daily basis: hedge fund managers, high frequency traders (who use high-speed computers to auto-trade in milliseconds at fractions of a cent), bloggers, newsletter spammers, TV personalities, pumpers (those who artificially inflate a stock's value within message boards and chat rooms, shorts (those whose best is hedged on the stock falling in value who continuously bash a stock with negative opinion), etc. There is so much misinformation that it is easy to be misled. During the recession, all of the experts were wasting their time trying to figure out if it would be a V (sharp), U (gradual), or W (an up-and-down) recovery. They pulled out large chunks of their money, while Buffett was investing in undervalued stocks at basement prices. Buffett's success is no coincidence. He is so good at value investing, that he's been doing it for half a century. Buffett follows a simple formula of investing in businesses he understands, with a low P/E (price-to-earnings) ratio, and a high Earnings Yield (Fontinelle, A. (2014, para. 4-5) [27]. According to the articles *30 Years Ago Warren Buffett Gave Away The Secret To Good Investing And Correctly Predicated No One Would Listen*, by Myles Udland of the BusinessInsider.com, Buffett explained in a 1984 speech at the Columbia Business School that:

The common intellectual theme of the investors from Graham-and-Doddsville is this: they search for discrepancies between the value of a business and the price of small pieces of that business in the market. And that's pretty much it. Buffett doesn't think about buying a stock; he thinks about buying a business. In Buffett's essay, he asks readers to consider a group of investors who outperformed the S&P 500 year in and year out. "In this group of successful investors that I want to consider," Buffett writes, "there has been a common intellectual patriarch, Ben Graham ... They have gone to different places and bought and sold different stocks and companies, yet they have a combined record that simply can't be explained by random chance." Buffett explains that the investors of Graham-and-Doddsville don't care when they buy stocks, or worry about a stock's beta or the "covariance in returns among securities." He says these investors are businessmen buying pieces of businesses, not traders buying stocks. Buffett concludes his essay by writing that some may wonder why he is giving away this basic investment philosophy of a number of investors who have outperformed the market. Isn't he just giving away the secret? "I can only tell you that the secret has been out for 50 years," Buffett writes, "...yet I have seen no trend toward value investing in the 35 years I've practiced it.

There seems to be some perverse human characteristic that likes to make easy things difficult. The academic world, if anything, has actually backed away from the teaching of value investing over the last 30 years. It's likely to stay that way. Ships will sail around the world but the Flat Earth Society will flourish. There will continue to be wide discrepancies between price and value in the marketplace, and those who read their Graham & Dodd will continue to prosper."[28]

Outside of Buffett's value investment strategy, below are some additional parameters and tips to becoming a successful stock investor:

• Don't lose – This is the number one (obvious) goal of professional investors; however, the rationale behind it may be slightly more complex than it appears. I am going to elaborate in two examples with percentages. In example one, you invest $10,000 into a stock with great news, but not much substance. Shortly thereafter, you're investment drops 50%, or down to $5,000. At this point, you now need to make 100% on your remaining investment, just to get back to where you started. 100%! The best stock portfolios may generate 10-12% per year, thus 100% is extremely difficult to accomplish. In example two, you only have $100 to invest; however, the brokerage firm you choose charges $10 per trade. Immediately you are down 10% in your investment, meaning you now need to make at least 20%

just to get back to even. Focus on the percentages and always invest conservatively. Make it your goal to prevent substantial percentage losses.

• Use all available resources – I like to use Marketwatch.com, as well as Finance.Yahoo.com (Yahoo Finance), to easily track my portfolio. I stay up-to-date on news with SeekingAlpha.com and CNBC on TV. I use Finviz.com to screen for high volume stocks with low P/E ratios, a dividend, a small percentage of shorts (people betting against my potential investment), and near the 52-week low. I also like to look at IPOScoop.com for up-to-date information on upcoming Initial Public Offerings (IPOs), as well as current statistics on recent IPOs.

• Diversify – Putting all of your eggs into one basket is a disaster waiting to happen. You have to diversify to mitigate risk. The further you diversify the further you lessen your risk. Putting the bulk or your entire investment into one stock is a high-risk scenario, which you cannot afford to lose. How many people have you ever heard of that invested all of their money into one stock only and hit it big? I don't know anyone like this, because the odds of that happening are pretty low. You're not going to get rich overnight, but that is okay. Build your portfolio with a solid foundation. Nobody wants to live in a penthouse propped up by toothpicks.

• Look for dividend-stocks first – One of the easiest ways of making passive income is through investment in stocks, which pay a dividend. Build a portfolio of dividend stocks, and reap the yearly rewards. It is up to you whether you choose to reinvest.

• Always follow the chart – The most successful stock investors study the chart. What you need to look for in a stock chart is a downward trend that has approached a slight rebound with a gradual increase in volume. Filter for stocks within 5 – 10% of their 52-week low. This is what the experts look for.

• Track high volume stocks – The last investment you want to make is one into a stock with declining or little to no volume. If you ever need to sell your shares, you may not be able to, and you'll find yourself stuck. I've had this happen first hand trading penny stocks numerous times.

• Never throw good money after bad – Have you ever heard of the stock strategy to average down? The parameters of the concept are that upon your initial investment, the stock goes down in value. In order to lessen the loss, you reinvest more money at the lower price, to in turn lower your average buy-in price. Though great in theory, this strategy is a recipe for disaster. It's very easy to get caught up averaging down again, and again, in order to lessen your loss. Before you know it, you've erased all of the profits from your portfolio, and the stock may very well continue to drop. Think of buying a car that turns out to be a lemon. It's in the shop constantly, causing you to throw more and more money into it, while all along you know you just need to dump it. Well, stocks can be lemons too. Only invest more if the stock goes up.

• Never get emotionally attached to a stock – Be objective, rather than subjective. Stick with the fundamentals of the chart and balance sheet, rather than the hype of a new product or service. They all say they're going to the moon, because if they didn't nobody would invest.

• Never persuade friends or family to invest in a stock – Advising a friend or family member on stock investment may be one of the quickest ways to fracture a relationship. The odds of predicting one stock that is going to the moon against all odds is like picking winning lottery numbers. It could happen, however, the odds of it happening are very small. The more likely scenario is that you may cost someone else his or her investment, which could leave a large pothole in their portfolio if they have not diversified. Are you going to reimburse them if/when your advice doesn't pan out? I didn't think so.

• Be wary of day trading – Day trading will always be high risk because of the outside factors that the average investor is up against. Market makers, high-frequency traders, and insiders within the companies you are investing in, can easily manipulate a stock; they do it on a regular basis. Market makers trade in the stock before the opening bell just to turn your nerves into an emotional roller coaster. They make a stock look like it's going straight to the moon or plummeting to the floor, in hopes that you either buy or sell at the worst possible time for you and the best possible time for them. High frequency traders have vastly lopsided the playing field by using computers to trade in and out of a stock within fractions of a second. I like to equate high frequency trading to when IBM's supercomputer, Watson, competed on *Jeopardy!* against two former champions. Watson dominated the competition without challenge due to superior computation abilities and easily took home the million-dollar prize. [29] Many penny stocks also pump up their values through news releases that make their businesses sound much better than they actually are. They claim they are on the verge of changing the world, and that "big news" is just around the corner. It reminds me of when someone tells you: "the check is in the mail." What usually happens is that these news releases are fabricated to inflate the stock as best as they can to make it go on a run. When the financials finally come out, all of the news is proven to be bunk. The owners (or officers if there are any) are suddenly rich, and often get away with you investment.

• Don't buy the index share hype – Index shares are becoming more and more common as a volatile opportunity for shorts to take advantage of novice investors with a smoke and mirrors show. For example, I recently followed an index share that was marketed as bear shares on the value of gold, meaning if gold went down in value, this stock should go up. Shortly thereafter, gold went down in value. Guess what the stock did? The index share plummeted (15-20% each day for an entire week). So, why did the index share go down when the entire marketing premise of the fund was contrary to what was happening? The answer is very simple: this fund, just like all of the rest of the index shares, has more people betting against it (shorts), than for it. Whether it is a volatility index (VIX) or gold index (bull or bear shares), neither is based upon sound investing.

• Don't have faith in the Securities and Exchange Commission (SEC) to be your safety net – You need to be aware of the inherent risks within stock investing. Anytime large sums of money are involved in anything, you will always find someone willing to do anything to take that money. The SEC will never have the resources to police them all, nor does the government want that level of scrutiny. At some point, money talks, and that is just the world we live in. How the SEC can continue to allow high frequency trading alone is a complete disservice to the average investor. If and when the SEC does make an actual arrest for insider trading, you should have no faith that justice will ever be served, or that you will ever recover your stolen investment. Cases brought by the SEC often become class action lawsuits, where they'll update you often on court proceedings as if it matters. At the end of the day, you can plan to recover next to nothing. The only solace the SEC can bring is an arrest.

Bonds

Bonds are one of the staples of any investment portfolio. Defined by Wikipedia (2014, para. 2): "A bond is a form of loan or IOU (sounded "I owe you"): the *holder* of the bond is the lender (creditor), the *issuer* of the bond is the borrower (debtor), and the *coupon* is the interest." [30] There are many different types of bonds. Bonds are most commonly used to finance government projects or government-backed mortgages. Within the private industry, corporate bonds are issued to bankroll long-term investments, etc. Per the WIkiHow.com article, *How to Invest in Bonds* (2014, Step 4, para. 2-9, Step 15, para. 1-3), the following bonds are the most common investment vehicles:

> • Debentures (or unsecured bonds) - The most common type of taxable bonds. All corporate bonds not otherwise pledged assets or properties are debentures.

> • Mortgage bonds - Pledge specific corporate property as collateral for the bond issued. In case the bond issuer defaults on either interest or principal payment, the mortgaged property may be sold to pay the bond bearers.

> • Ginnie Mae bonds and mortgaged-backed securities (MBS) - are shares in federally backed home mortgages. As homeowners repay their mortgages, the proceeds are

divided up and paid to the bondholders until the mortgage is paid off.

• Convertible bonds - Bonds that are convertible to a specified number of common shares of the same corporation.

• Treasury bonds - Issued by the Treasury and backed by the federal government. Treasury bonds have no credit risk because of the federal government's ability to print money.

• Tax-free bonds or municipal bonds - Issued by cities, counties, states, and other government agencies, and are free of federal taxes. These bonds are best for investors in the highest tax brackets to invest in taxable accounts.

• Zero-coupon bonds defer all interest payments until maturity. Zero-coupon bonds are most suitable for retirement accounts. [31]

In order to properly invest in bonds, you will need to institute a strategy for bond buying. A sound strategy will be defined by the following parameters:

The best time to buy bonds is when the prices are low. Bond prices are lowest when the interest rate peaks. That is the ideal time to buy because you benefit not only from better yields, but also from capital gains when interest rates start to decline. Interest rate tends to peak when short-term rates equal or exceed long-term rates, creating an **inverted yield curve**, a rare opportunity to buy bonds at great prices. [31]

Additionally, the percentage you invest in bonds should be based upon your age.

A rough rule of thumb is that your age should equal the percentage of your assets in bonds and fixed income, and the rest in stocks. For example, if you are 25, you should have 25% assets in bonds, and 75% in stocks. If you are 55, you should have 55% bonds and 45% stocks. To mitigate interest rate risk, build a bond ladder consisting of short and intermediate term bonds maturing one year after another. For example, if you have $50,000 to invest in bonds, invest $10,000 each in bonds maturing in 1 year, 2 years, 3 years, 4 years, and 5 years. When the shortest-term bond matures after one year, reinvest the proceeds in a new bond maturing in 5 years. Repeat this every year, so your bond portfolio always contains five bonds, maturing one year after another. Bond laddering is a sound investment strategy because short term bonds are less sensitive to interest rate fluctuations, and should interest rate rise, you have the opportunity to reinvest in a higher-yielding bond as your bonds mature. [31]

In order to officially invest in bonds you have the option to either purchase them through banks or directly through the Federal Reserve. When purchasing through a bank however, be mindful that there will be potential fees associated with the purchase of each bond. If you choose to buy treasury bonds through the Federal Reserve, you can go straight to www.treasurydirect.gov.

Mutual Funds

When investing in a retirement account, one of the best options available is to purchase shares of a mutual fund. Per CNN Money (2014):

> A mutual fund pools money from hundreds and thousands of investors to construct a portfolio of stocks, bonds, real estate, or other securities, according to its charter. Examples are: growth funds, which buy shares of burgeoning companies; sector funds, which buy shares of companies in a particular sector, such as technology or health care; and index funds, which buy shares of every stock in a particular index, such as the S&P 500. [32]

In order to properly invest in mutual funds it is important that you set parameters. First, you will need to assess the risk of the investments within a particular fund. Look to see whether the mutual fund meets your criteria for investment. Is the fund weighted more heavily in stocks, bonds, active, or passive? Next, try to verify how many percentage points the fund charges per year, in addition to whether or not you may incur taxes based on whether or not the stocks within a fund pay a dividend, or whether potential capital gains taxes may be incurred due to the fund manager selling stock. Make sure that you track mutual funds for long-term consistency, as they are a long-term investment. Short-term winners have the potential to be losers long-term, thus it is important to know the history of a fund. It is also important to actively track your funds. A mutual fund with a long-term downward trend is not a fund you want to be invested in. Ultimately, when looking to invest in mutual funds, look first to invest in index funds due to the various advantages. Per CNN Money: "Index funds tend to charge lower expenses and be more tax efficient, and there's no risk the fund manager will make sudden changes that throw off your portfolio's allocation." [32]

With the proper investment strategy and parameters, mutual funds may ultimately be one of the easiest investments you can make in your portfolio.

Our Story – The Inexperienced Investor Pothole

- **Situation** – I had always been fascinated by the stock market, yet never really had any money to invest in it. From the time I took my first finance class in high school where we mock-purchased stocks and built a portfolio, I found it engaging to track the rise and fall of stocks. I also found the culture of Wall Street to be appealing due to the absurd sums of money that they could seem to generate in an afternoon. Who wouldn't want to make a million dollars in a couple of hours? Upon obtaining employment for my first real job after college, I was suddenly making lots of money. My salary dwarfed anything I had made up to that point, and it felt awesome. After working for the first six months or so, I found myself with lots of money and nothing exciting to spend it on. I also had lots of free time, as I was on call, so naturally I started watching MSNBC. Within a few days of watching the market, I decided I wanted in. I convinced myself needed a "hobby" (or a gambling addiction) anyway, and if I really could make big money, maybe I could quit my job.
- **Task** – Become a day trader. Make big money and quit my day job.

• **Action** – At one point prior to my investment account, I had received a mailer about a penny stock that was destined for greatness. I tracked that stock for a couple of months, up and through a run that it made. Unfortunately, I never had the money to invest, as this was before my first real job. I felt like I missed an opportunity, and was therefore determined that this time around; I wasn't going to miss the run. I figured by investing large sums of money into penny stocks, all the stock had to do was move up a few pennies, or fractions of a penny, and in an instant I was up hundreds. The risk-to-reward factor was like a drug. I did my research, read the message boards, and finally settled on one, which I knew was going to go big time. It was a stock fabricated around building material supply in Dubai, UAE. At the time (2006), Dubai was going through the biggest building boom on the planet. It was transforming a sleepy nomadic beach and desert territory on the Persian Gulf into an epicenter of luxury condominiums, residences, office buildings, hotels, and extra's. Dubai was trying to convert its economy from oil to technology. It was like New York City on steroids, yet nobody lived there to support the infrastructure. They imported labor from India and Asia, while the building materials were imported from all over the planet. Since Dubai is in the desert, they had to import. The company I was following was based in North America, and had contracts to supply building materials, thus my investment seemed like a no-brainer. I sank the bulk of my money into the stock. I was convinced it couldn't fail. Next, I committed a cardinal sin of investing and told my father (a family member) about it. I convinced him to take out an equity line of credit for $40,000, as this was a sure thing; we couldn't lose. We split the loan $20,000 each. I invested my entire half into the stock, which was also another cardinal sin of investing (not diversifying). Shortly after, and without notice, my day job required me to leave my investment center and go to our corporate office for a week of training. As fate would have it, one of the days that I was in the office, the stock made its one and only run to the moon. Unable to check my account until lunchtime, I logged into one of the computers in our corporate hallway and saw that I was up $36,000! I had no idea what to do. My nerves were through the roof and my heart was racing. Inexperienced in investing and overanalyzing my options, I couldn't make a decision. Should I sell? Or would it go higher? I completely clammed up. I decided I couldn't focus on it, until I could get back to my room and log into my personal computer to sell.

• **Result** – That evening when I got back to my hotel room, I logged into the computer. Astonished, the stock had not only risen, as I had seen it earlier in the day, but it had also plummeted that afternoon, when I wasn't able to track it. It was basically like a firework; it built up to the very moment that it exploded and took off as high as it could before it ran out of fuel. What I found now was the burnt-out shell. I lost everything. My gains were erased along with my entire investment.

• **Takeaway** – At the time of my penny stock catastrophe I committed numerous cardinal sins of investing. I also didn't have the experience to be playing around with the kind of money I was playing around with. Yes, I was studying charts, reading finance articles, and watching MSNBC, but I still didn't know when to sell. I was also emotionally attached to one stock that, like 99% of all penny stocks, was all talk and no substance. I knew the stock would make a run, but I didn't know it was one-and-done. My father and I were left owing $40,000. I ended up writing off my stock loss for next three years on my taxes. The guilt I feel over the whole experience is more than humbling. Not only did I lose a lot of money that wasn't even mine, but also I really let my dad down.

Conclusion

Inside the walls of one of the companies I used to work for, we always used to hear the phrase: "we wouldn't be anywhere if it weren't for our investments." I truly believe the company statement was one hundred percent correct. When times were tough we would rely on those investments, and when times were great, those investments were icing on the cake. Debt management and conservative finances are what keep you out of debt, whereas investments are where you truly build wealth.

It is also important to understand that the vast majority of investments are not get-rich-quick schemes. Investing takes patience, commitment, and reinvestment. Reinvesting your profits into new investments can only increase your portfolio, while furthering your net worth. Take advantage of investment opportunities when they arise, when the timing is right, and remember that if the timing is wrong, there will always be another investment opportunity. Always, always, always diversify.

Avoid saving for the sake of saving, and further your investments instead. Give saving a purpose, such as an emergency fund, or your next vehicle. Without a purpose, saving just to save is counterintuitive due to inflation. Look at the rate of inflation versus the rate on your savings account. The same methodology applies to investments that may not be worth your money, such as CDs. CDs are sure things, and because they are, they have very low rates. In my opinion, CDs should come into your portfolio after more substantial investments have been made.

When it comes to investments: invest, collect, and reinvest. Change your life forever.

Money Tips

• Create an emergency fund with a goal of $1,000. Once you have established your emergency fund, and paid off your debt, place an additional $9,000 into liquid investments. If at some point you ever lose your job, or have a significant life-event occur, you will have $10,000 readily available to you.

• Start a personal business. File your LLC, buy a domain name, and build a website. Advertise your business on your vehicle and write off all of your expense. Enjoy the benefits of owning your own business.

• Invest in others and become the bank. Select and evaluate the risks (or borrowers), and build a portfolio, which will pay in excess of 10% interest. Set yearly goals to increase the interest amount.

• Buy a rental property or properties and build cash flow. View rental income as your new retirement plan.

• Invest in conventional retirement savings, post rental property. Select mutual funds (stocks or bonds). Assess long-term results and projections, and make your selections.

THE TAX CODE

Why do we all dread tax season? Is it because we feel anxiety due to the accuracy of our taxes? Is the Internal Revenue Service (IRS) one audit away from finding out that we didn't pay for something? Or maybe we have taken one too many deductions, and feel we may owe a large amount of money. Maybe we don't have the money to pay the tax bill? Or, then again, maybe we feel that we've already paid our fair share; and we don't approve of where those tax dollars are going. Regardless of what the surface reason is, the underlying reason we dread taxes is that we don't fully understand the tax code. Just as a cat or dog is fearful of a loud vacuum cleaner, we are fearful of taxes for the same reason: we don't understand taxes. Unlike the cat or dog however, who will probably never realize that the vacuum (though loud), is actually cleaning the floor; we are able to learn and master the tax code.

For most people, doing their own taxes can be a very intimidating task. With the complexity and intricacies of a tax code that changes yearly with a vote this way or that way, many simply take their tax documents to someone else for processing. Reasons for passing the buck can be as simple as not knowing how to process and submit taxes, to knowing how to submit taxes, but not wanting to deal with process altogether. Some people prefer to use tax professionals only, for the purpose of placing the "burden" (or more importantly, the liability) on them.

Ways to Make Taxes Work for You

How many wealthy people do you know who simply give up control and drop off all of their tax documents at the nearest business willing to file for them? The answer is not many. Most wealthy people hire skilled accountants, who study the ins and outs, and know exactly where to take advantage of the tax code. You may call what an accountant does with loopholes and breaks as cheating the system, but the reality is that the vast majority are playing within the parameters of the game; they're just better at it than you or I. Mastering taxes takes practice, just as any other skill that you might hope to learn—and mastery of the various ways to make taxes work for you is a skill that you can no longer ignore.

Personal Business

One of the best and easiest ways to make taxes work for you (rather than against you) is by starting a personal business. Aside from the rewarding benefits of self-empowerment and being your own boss, owning your own business can bring you great tax benefits that the tax code was specifically designed to give you. The federal government specifically promotes small business in hopes that your business contributes to the economy by providing jobs. If your chosen business does not provide jobs, you are still contributing to the overall economy and are provided various breaks. The reason for writing a tax code that promotes small business is really a simple concept when you think about it.

Your background, experiences, developed skillset, personal interests, and lofty goals will guide you onto one path or another. Open multiple businesses and diversify just as you would with your portfolio by minimizing the risk of having all of your eggs in one basket. What resources are available to you? Do you have a friend or family member that could guide you? If you do, great; if not, start anyway. Create your own path by doing your own research and being resourceful. Based on the path(s) you decide to pursue, examples of your business opportunity could be any one of the following:

- Consulting business – Finance, insurance, military, life coach, etc.

- Freelance business – Examples are wedding photography, creating virtual tours for homes, which are listed for sale, journalism, author, teaching music lessons, etc.

- Franchise – Open a business with a proven business model. Make sure the location can support your store, and then apply the business model.

- Web-based business – Blogs, E-commerce, hosting hubs, or service-based business such as recruiting or training, etc.

- Provide a service – Personal Trainer/Nutritionist, Massage Therapist, Real Estate Agent, property management business, maintenance business (lawn service, pool service, pest control, painting), etc.

- Retail business – Bakery, furniture store, distillery, etc.

Upon choosing a business or businesses, it is time to create a business plan, start your LLC and get organized. A typical LLC can be filed for around $300 – $500, or less. Many web-based filing businesses already exist which will submit all of the documentation for you, such as: RocketLawyer.com, LegalZoom.com, MyCorporation.com, etc. Keep records of everything. For a website, secure a domain name from GoDaddy.com or NameCheap.com, then pursue web design. Two resources that are great for finding a web design service, which will meet your needs, are: SiteBuilderReport.com or TopSEOs.com.

Keep track of your expenses. Every single expense, which is related to your business, you will need to track. Common personal business-related expenses are:

- Auto – Purchasing vehicle(s), Maintenance, Mileage, Parking/Tolls
- Business-related travel – keep all receipts and invoices
- Costs of goods sold
- Depreciation
- Fees – Accounting, Credit Card, Franchise, Monthly Overhead
- Inventory – products to sell, vehicles
- Insurance – Group, Health, Worker's Compensation
- Maintenance
- Office – Home Office, Office Rent
- Startup Fees – Costs to file the LLC, secure a domain name, web design, etc.
- Utilities – Electricity, Internet, Phone (cellular or landline)

Having a personal business is one of the best and most proven ways to lower your tax bill by changing your statement from in the red to in the black. As long as you keep organized records, you will be able to write off and deduct a significant amount expenses and easily lower your tax bracket. Make sure that you have physical copies of everything you are claiming though, as one of the leading triggers of IRS audits is a personal business, which does not report making any income. Back up your claims by keeping organized records (paper and Excel reports), as well as being prepared.

Become a Landlord

After starting a personal business and filing an LLC, the second-most advantageous tax-incentive strategy is purchasing rental property (due to the many tax deductions available to landlords). In order to promote housing, the tax code is written to provide great benefits to landlords by giving incentives to those who provide housing. Per Fishman, S. (2014, para. 3-18), the *Top Ten Deductions for Landlords* are:

• Interest – Mortgage interest payments on loans used to acquire or improve rental property and interest on credit cards for goods or services used in a rental activity.

• Depreciation – The actual cost of a house, apartment building, or other rental property is not fully deductible in the year in which you pay for it. Instead, landlords get back the cost of real estate through depreciation. This involves deducting a portion of the cost of the property over several years.

• Repairs – The cost of repairs to rental property (provided the repairs are ordinary, necessary, and reasonable in amount) are fully deductible in the year in which they are incurred. Good examples of deductible repairs include repainting, fixing gutters or floors, fixing leaks, plastering, and replacing broken windows.

• Local Travel – Landlords are entitled to a tax deduction whenever they drive anywhere for their rental activity. You can: deduct your actual expenses (gasoline, upkeep, repairs), or use the standard mileage rate (56 cents per mile for 2014; 56.5 cents per mile for 2013). To qualify for the standard mileage rate, you must use the standard mileage method the first year you use a car for your business activity.

• Long Distance Travel – If you travel overnight for your rental activity, you can deduct your airfare, hotel bills, meals, and other expenses. IRS auditors closely scrutinize deductions for overnight travel, and many taxpayers get caught claiming these deductions without proper records to back them up.

• Home Office – This deduction applies not only to space devoted to office work, but also to a workshop or any other home workspace you use for your rental business.

• Employees and Independent Contractors – Whenever you hire anyone to perform services for your rental activity, you can deduct their wages as a rental business expense.

• Casualty and Theft Losses – If your rental property is damaged or destroyed from a sudden event like a fire or flood, you may be able to obtain a tax deduction for all or part of your loss. How much you may deduct depends on how much of your property was destroyed and whether the loss was covered by insurance.

• Insurance – You can deduct the premiums you pay for almost any insurance for your rental activity. This includes fire, theft, and flood insurance for rental property, as well as landlord liability insurance. If you have employees, you can deduct the cost of their health and workers' compensation insurance.

• Legal and Professional Services – You can deduct fees that you pay to attorneys, accountants, property management companies, real estate investment advisors, and other professionals. You can deduct these fees as operating expenses as long as the fees are paid for work related to your rental activity. [33]

Employment-Related Expenses

Believe it or not, the tax code is written so that there are actually a few employment-related expenses, which you can deduct. The catch, though, with any employment-related expense, is that your employer cannot have already reimbursed you for the expense. Examples of employment-related expenses are:

• Business-Related Meals (which were not reimbursed) – an example would be a working lunch, or meals on a business trip. You will not be able to deduct the alcoholic beverages you had, which were provided complimentary at the hotel pool.

• Moving – Deduct transportation, storage expenses (up to 30 days), and the cost to travel to the new location. In order to claim the moving expenses deduction however, the move must be greater than 50 miles, and time test requirements must be met after the move. Per Turbotax.intuit.com (2014):

> You must work full-time for a minimum of 39 weeks during the initial 12-month period that starts on the day you arrive in the new location. You can still satisfy this requirement when the 39 weeks are not consecutive and even when it's for multiple employers. The IRS does not specify the number of days or hours you must work each

week to be a full-time employee; instead, it defers to your industry's commonly accepted standard. [34]

• Job-hunting – looking for potential employment, you can deduct expenses. Per the article, *Job hunting could help cut taxes*, by Bell, K. (2013) you can write off:

• Employment and outplacement agency fees

• Resume services

• Printing and mailing costs of search letters

• Want-ad placement fees

• Telephone calls

• Travel expenses, including out-of-town job-hunting trips. [35]

Interest Expenses

Build your debt management strategy around knowing which interest you can and cannot write off. Pay off the interest, which serves no benefit to your taxes. Examples of interest items, which you can deduct per the tax code, include:

• Mortgage Interest

• Student Loan Interest

• Home Equity Interest

- Interest on money borrowed to purchase investment property
- Interest related to business-expenses

Examples of personal interest items, which you cannot deduct per the tax code, include:

- Credit Card Interest
- Auto Loan Interest

When Congress enacted the Tax Reform Act of 1986, the personal interest deduction, which applied to credit card and car loan interest, could longer be claimed. Per Turbotax.intuit.com, Intuit Inc. (2013):

> According to the Treasury Department, the personal interest deduction was seen as encouraging Americans to spend money rather than save it; in reality, it also reduced tax revenues. That's because money that people put in savings earned them interest, which was taxable income, but if they ran up credit card debt, they could deduct the interest from their income, which lowered their tax liability. [36]

Dependents

Per the article, *Average cost to raise a kid: $241,080* (Hicken, M. 2013, para. 2):

> It will cost an estimated $241,080 for a middle-income couple to raise a child born last year for 18 years, according to a U.S. Department of Agriculture report. That's up almost 3% from 2011 and doesn't even include the cost of college." [37]

Assuming that the cost increases by 3% a year, or roughly the rate of inflation, the cost of having dependents has never been greater, and will also never be lower than it is right now. The tax code is written to provide breaks from the expenses of raising or housing dependents. Some of those credits or deductions are:

• $1000 credit per dependent

• Option to potentially write off medical expenses within a certain limit for a disabled child

• Daycare (including Summer Camp, Nannies, and Babysitters)

Charitable Donations

We all have random piles of stuff lying around our houses. Whether it is clothes, household items, cars, boats, etc., we all have something that we don't use that at the same time, we don't know what to do with. You could have a garage sale and give away your items at a fraction of their actual value to bargain hunters, or you could donate those same items for their real value. I personally love the option of donating, because I not only can write off those donations for the actual value of the items I am donating, but it also makes me feel good knowing that someone else is getting a great piece of furniture or pair of pants at a great price. You can donate anything from clothing, household items, or furniture, all the way to vehicles. Each year, we personally donate a couple thousand dollars worth of items. In the past we have donated fine china, our couch and loveseat, my entire CD collection of nearly 1,000 CDs, nearly 200 spa robes, etc. I don't regret any of those donations, as we were later able to write them off, as well as make someone's day in the meantime.

It is also very easy now to donate to charitable causes for response efforts involving significant weather events around the world. From the tsunamis in Thailand or Japan, to the earthquake in Haiti, or the destruction in New Orleans due to Hurricane Katrina, the Red Cross has been there to accept donations on behalf of the victims of the tragedy. You also have the option to often donate at your local grocery store or fast food restaurant to the charities that they support. Some places ask if you would like to round up your bill to the nearest dollar, while others ask for a full dollar. Each charitable donation is tax deductible and will make you feel great.

If you want to find an extensive list of organizations, just charitable perform a simple Google search, and you will find that you have options all around you. Some of the organizations we have used in the past include:

- Goodwill
- Betty Griffin House
- Boys and Girls Club
- Red Cross
- Salvation Army

Our story – The Tax Pothole

• **Situation** – When a couple I know first got married, they decided to combine their incomes and try to pay off their house. They each brought in over $65,000, and within a few years paid off the house in full. Relieved to no longer have a mortgage payment, they quickly assumed they were in the clear. What they didn't realize though was that now they had even less to deduct from their taxes. Their first tax bill after paying off the home exceeded $4,000.

• **Task** – Lower their tax burden by investing in credits and deductibles.

• **Action** – Since paying off the house, my buddy and his wife decided to start a family. She left her job and became a stay-at-home mom, cutting their earned income in half. They had a baby, and they started a personal business. They also regularly donate.

• **Result** – Their family can now deduct all of their personal business-related expenses. They deduct mileage, as well as business meals. They can deduct additional utility costs, a portion of his cell phone bill, etc. They can also claim their child for the tax credit, as well as deduct their charitable donations.

- **Takeaway** – Sometimes, removing all of your debt can leave you with a large tax bill, if you haven't planned to offset it. It is essential to invest in a personal business, as well as charitable donations. Rental properties, as well as having dependents, can also help you to lessen your tax burden.

Conclusion

I hope this chapter has opened your eyes to see that the tax highway isn't all that bad. There are plenty of credits and deductions to go around, which you can capitalize on just as easily as the next person. Stop overpaying. Do you consider yourself a bargain shopper? Would you go to the store during a sale, with a handful of coupons, ignore the sale racks, and insist on paying full price? Can you realistically think of anywhere where you would willingly volunteer to overpay? I can't. Don't overpay your taxes. Pay what you legitimately owe within the code and not a penny more.

Remember, there's a reason why many people and corporations pay lower tax rates than you or I; they employ the best accountants. It's the New York Yankees versus an AAA farm team. If you employed the best accountants, you would also pay the lowest tax rates. It's like being jealous of the best athlete in a particular sport; you want what they have because to you it appears effortless on their part, while in reality you are overlooking the years of practice that it took them to get where they are.

Your goal should be to master the application of the tax code, while continuing to fine-tune your personal investment strategy. You can avoid learning the tax code, and always pay more than you should be, or you can master the tax code, and make it work for you and your investments. Fortunately, for us, easily accessible resources are available from Turbotax.com, HRBlock.com, TaxACt.com, TaxSlayer.com, etc.

As the old saying goes: "there are only two things in this world that are unavoidable: death and taxes." Though still true to this day, the way you choose to live is up to you, just as the way you choose to pay taxes is up to you. While many folks become nervous with anxiety each year at tax time, others welcome it. Hold yourself accountable and put some effort into mastering the ins and outs of the tax code. In the end, you'll be glad that you did.

Money Tips

• Start a personal business and file an LLC. Reap the benefits in your taxes.

• Become a landlord by purchasing rental property and deduct the expenses.

• Take an interest in your taxes and do them yourself. Use online software such as Turbotax.com, HRBlock.com, etc.

• Start donating. Take old items, which are just collecting dust around your home, and donate them to a charitable organization. It feels good and you will get the deduction for your taxes.

• Get the $1,000 credit per dependent, and write off your childcare expenses.

IMPLEMENTATION

Truly mastering personal finance takes an active approach. The point of no return is now, and your future is up to you. You can choose to follow the road map to the real American dream with the knowledge you've learned in this book, or you can choose to drive blind. Do you drive your car to work with your eyes closed?

It's easy to carelessly go on buying whatever is sold to you, rather than choosing what is truly in your best interest. If you choose to commit to the journey, you need to understand is that it is not going to be easy. Avoiding temptation is extremely difficult. Every day we are bombarded with ads, solicitations, and sales people with great pitches, selling wonderful products and services that we want. Sometimes your personal finance vehicle is going to have to slow down to a snail's pace in order to avoid all of the temptation (or potholes). Paying off debt and avoiding temptation is hard, which is why you always need to remember your end goal. Think of the view at the end of the road. Think of driving cross-country to the best beach, with the whitest sand, the bluest water, the greatest amenities, and all of your friends and family are waiting there to throw an epic party. You can make it! Keep in perspective, though, that unique challenges lie ahead.

The Personal/Professional Seesaw

When assessing your finances, it is always important to be mindful of balance. There are parameters you should work within to accomplish your goals. I like to think of the personal/professional seesaw concept, which essentially means that you cannot focus solely on one side, because if you do, the other will touch the ground. You have to keep both sides in constant motion, which is very much a metaphor for life; that if you focus too much on finances or money, your family life is going to take a dive. Bryan Dyson, former CEO of Coca Cola, has said:

> Imagine life as a game in which you are juggling some five balls in the air. You name them - work, family, health, friends and spirit and you're keeping all of these in the air. You will soon understand that work is a rubber

ball. If you drop it, it will bounce back. But the other four balls - family, health, friends and spirit are made of glass. If you drop one of these, they will be irrevocably scuffed, marked, nicked, damaged or even shattered. They will never be the same. You must understand that and strive for balance in your life. [38]

Think of all of the kids out there from wealthy households who constantly act out because their parents don't pay any attention to them or constantly pass them off. They may have what appears on the outside to be a fancy finance vehicle, but truthfully inside the vehicle is just a shell – or hollow. Do yourself and your family a favor and be mindful of balance.

Support

Accomplishing a goal like going on a journey to the land to financial freedom is very difficult by yourself, and even more so when a member or members of your family disagrees with your plan. In order to set your family and yourself up for success, you have to accomplish your financial goals together. Map out the journey. Know where the turns, bumps, and slow areas are going to be. Teach your spouse, kids, parents, and friends what you have learned, and commit to the plan as a unit with momentum.

From my experience, getting everyone on the same page can sometimes be quite challenging, as interests change and your lives evolve; however, part of working within your family dynamic is that you may have to compromise on your personal goals in order to accomplish the goals of the group. Besides, what would be the point of throwing your party living debt free in the land of financial freedom, if you had nobody to share the experience with? Combine your income and philosophy. Journey ahead together.

Conclusion

Are you ready to get ahead? Are you psyched up to start living your new life, free of financial burden? To evict your student loans and credit card debt from your life forever? Are you ready to live your life carefree, with the cash to do what you want, when you want to do it? Can you picture the stress leaving you forever? Can you see yourself on the beach with the white sand and the blue water? Can you picture the party you are going to have? Can you picture yourself free?

I wrote this book to capture our experience with all of the ups, downs, and gray areas in between. We lived high on the hog, until the day reality caught up and gave us a stern kick in the pants. All the potholes we drove through left us with a clunker we didn't know how to fix. We were broken down, in the middle of nowhere, and without any lifelines for guidance. I honestly think living with debt is similar to living behind bars: short-term debt is the equivalent of an overnight jail stay; whereas long-term debt feels like an extended prison sentence for crimes you didn't realize you had committed.

Throughout the journey I've had numerous pride-swallowing moments. I've had my credit card declined in the grocery or department store. I've had the credit card company refuse to increase my borrowing limit. At one point, I was even on a work trip where we were checking into our company-booked hotel, and I couldn't secure the room, because I didn't have $150 available in credit or cash, for the typical incidental temporary hold charge. I told the hotel directly in front of 7-10 colleagues, that if they wouldn't make an exception, I was going to sleep in the rental car. It was embarrassing and truly upsetting. Luckily, the hotel made an exception.

Unfortunately, in order to live the life I'm selling in this book, you may go through your own pride-swallowing moments, potentially including bankruptcy. It is my hunch that most people don't willingly file for bankruptcy, thus if bankruptcy makes the most sense in your situation, you shouldn't feel guilty about it. If I had the choice to pick $100,000 in student loan debt (including a lifetime of repaying $500+ a month, in addition to garnished wages or social security) versus $100,000 in credit card debt, which I could wipe out short-term by filing for bankruptcy, the choice is a no-brainer. Additionally, nobody knows the cards, which you have been dealt in your life, thus the truth in others' judgment is that they should be looking in the mirror. It is my personal opinion that publicly posting bankruptcies is unethical and unfair, due to the various life events that can derail the finances of even the best so-called financial experts.

I wrote this book because of my background and because of how I grew up. My parents taught me the value of money by offering a weekly allowance for chores. I learned that if I completed my chores, my dad would pay me. My allowance rate was determined by how old I was, and when I had a birthday, I earned a raise. I became aware very early on that in order to buy the "really cool" things that I wanted, I would need to save my money. I became great at saving, often saving up hundreds or thousands. I never really knew what to put the money into though, and often spent it on depreciating assets, things like guitars or cars/car parts. I didn't have the first clue of how to properly invest the money, thus I spent it on things that brought no return. When I eventually moved away from home for college, I burned through my entire savings of $10,000, and went flat broke. I ran up my credit card and had to start selling my possessions just to pay the rent and eat. I made bad financial decisions for years.

When I wasn't spending my money on depreciating assets, I was gambling on penny stocks, where I lost thousands. I took out loans and financed my cars and house because that's all I knew. I didn't pay off debts because I had plenty of money coming in. I never realize I had a problem.

I focused on earned income, rather than unearned income. Instead of reading books on personal finance and capitalizing on the influx of income I was now making, I was busy wasting money and squandering the opportunity. As a result, I continue to pay the price now for years of bad financial decisions. Many of my current peers are living their lives debt and overhead free, while I have yet to start the race.

I realize now that there is not any one reason why I was lacking a financial education, but rather numerous reasons. My allowance that I earned as a young man was awesome, and I will forever be grateful to my dad for giving it to me. However, I realize though now that the model I learned early on was to be an employee. Including my yearly raises, what I knew is what steered me into earned income. Quite naturally, I have always worked for employers and tried to earn yearly raises, while branching out on my own (though enticing), has always felt foreign.

When I was younger, I never once read a book on personal finance. In fact, the only class I ever remember taking was the class where we tracked our mock stock portfolios. I didn't know anybody who owned and maintained rental property. I didn't ever see my parents' budget, debt management techniques, or tools. We never had family meetings about finance. I realize now though, that regardless of what was presented to me, I should have taken it upon myself to learn as much about personal finance as I could from the moment I had real money in my pocket.

I hope you find the information in this book useful, and that you will be able to apply it in some form to your own life. I usually look at any teaching material as worth it, if I even learned one thing that I didn't know beforehand. I've tried to encompass all that I know into this text, thus it is my hope you now know what to do in order to live your life overhead and pothole free. Start planning your party for when you reach the land of financial freedom, and make sure you never look back.

Money Tips – Greater Than / Less Than

• Financing a home with a thirty year FHA ARM loan < Renting to save up 20% toward a fifteen year fixed rate

    o An FHA loan has PMI for life, thus saving up a 20% down payment note only lets you avoid, PMI, but also gives you a standard loan product, free of government intervention. Always shoot for the shortest loan terms as possible and save yourself thousands.

• Pay off $5000 in credit card debt at 8.99% interest > Pay off $5000 in government-backed Student Loan debt at 6.8% interest

   o Paying off credit cards, should take some priority over paying off student loans, because at least with student loan debt you can write off the interest. On the other hand, student loans cannot be incorporated into a bankruptcy, and if you cannot pay, they will balloon in size. The government has the ability to garnish your wages and even your social security. Pick the lesser of two evils based on your situation.

• Financing college with student loans < Financing college by other means

   o Avoid government-backed student loans at all costs, as they are one of the worst loan products ever created. The federal government is well aware of the current 1.2 trillion dollar student loan balance, and has done nothing to provide relief to our students, or fix the problem. Look to scholarships, employment benefits, savings, or as a last ditch effort, credit cards. As written in the article, *I'm 57 and owe $152,000 in student loans* by Sheridan, P. (2014, para. 14) "due to the excessive interest rates (some exceeding 13%), the issue caught the attention of Senator

Elizabeth Warren, who introduced a bill earlier this year to allow millions of people like Anderson to refinance their student loans. However, the bill was blocked in June." [39]

- Government-backed loans (Student/FHA/etc.) < Private loans

  o Avoid government-backed home and student loans at every opportunity. Government-back loans are available to those who cannot obtain financing elsewhere. Because you are considered a high risk, the government hedges its investment in you, by providing the worst terms and conditions possible. At the end of day, the government will get its money back whether you actively pay it back or they just deduct it from you.

- Financing/leasing a new car from a car dealership < Purchasing a used car in cash from a private seller

  o By purchasing a used car you are avoiding the dealer fees, markup, maintenance plans, and sales commissions, which can add anywhere from $2000 or more to the cost of the car. Also by purchasing a car, which is at least five years old, it has already depreciated significantly, thus you are not paying for more than the car is worth. Make sure your purchase is in cash only and not financed.

- Zero overhead and cash purchases > Financing and payment plans o Buy your furniture, appliances, and any other products whose company offers a payment plan, with cash. There are years of data and overwhelming odds that you will not be able to pay off the balance within the zero interest window provided in the financing terms. The company is betting against you. Don't fall into the trap.

• Cash purchases > Credit purchases

o Cash purchases trump all credit card purchases (even cards which offer points). The reason why cash is supreme is that even if you pay off the credit card balance monthly to generate points toward gift cards and trips, at some point you could slip up, which is what the credit card company is betting on. The odds are against you. Additionally, why would you pay excessive rates if you didn't have to? According to the WallStCheatSheet.com article, *5 Worst Rates on Retailer Credit Cards* (2014), the worst retail credit card with the highest rate peaks at 28.99%, while the lowest is 9.99%. [40] My advice is ditch the cards, with the exception of one – for emergencies only, like when you forgot your cash, or your debit card doesn't work because the network is down (this actually happened to me in a restaurant).

• Invest in 401(k) < Invest in Rental Property

o Rental properties are the better investment due to the cash flow generated in unearned income. Though a 401(k) is tax-free (while the money is in the account, prior to age 65), you're betting on an unknown, that you will even live to retirement. A rental property could start paying you now. However, I also don't recommend leaving money on the table if your employer is offering a match. The bottom line is it is okay to invest in both, but give the rental property priority.

• Invest in dividend stocks > Invest in stocks without dividends

    o Though it may be enticing to invest in stocks without dividends, always remember that the stocks that do pay dividends are not only being held accountable with your investment, but they will also be the stocks, which build unearned income within your portfolio. As unearned income is your ultimate goal, it would be wise to invest in dividend stocks over those without dividends.

• Take your taxes to a tax processing business < Do your taxes yourself

    o Take an active approach, and invest in yourself by learning the parameters of the tax code. Various web-based businesses, as well as Internet "how to" articles, are readily available for anyone willing to learn.

• Starting a personal business > Working as a career employee

    o Start a personal business for the tax breaks alone. Be mindful that if you repay and remove all of your debt without offsetting the tax burden with a personal business or other means, you may owe Uncle Sam a few extra nickels at the end of the year.

- Earned Income < Unearned Income
    o Unearned (or passive) Income will always trump Earned Income, due the various tax breaks and incentives. In addition, would you rather make money for actively working, or make money for doing nothing? I think you know the answer.

BIBLIOGRAPHY

1. (2014). Sunstone (medieval). *Wikipedia.org*. Retrieved from http://en.wikipedia.org/wiki/Sunstone_(medieval)

2. Random House Dictionary, copyright Random House, Inc. (2014). *"Wealthy."* Retrieved from Dictionary.com http://dictionary.reference.com/browse/wealthy?s=t

3. (2014). Passive Income. *Wikipedia.org*. Retrieved from http://en.wikipedia.org/wiki/Passive_income

4. (2014). Elon Musk. *Wikipedia.org*. Retrieved from http://en.wikipedia.org/wiki/Elon_Musk

5. (2014). Richard Branson. *Wikipedia.org*. Retrieved from http://en.wikipedia.org/wiki/Richard_branson

6. (2014). Warren Buffett. *Wikipedia.org*. Retrieved from http://en.wikipedia.org/wiki/Warren_Buffett

7. McWhinnie, E. (2014, June 8). Are Americans Filling Up on Too Much Debt? *USAToday.com*. Retrieved from http://www.usatoday.com/story/money/personalfinance/2014/06/08/wscs-are-americans-filling-up-on-too-much-debt/10166869/

8. Green, D. (2013, May 31). Beat the New FHA MIP Cancellation Policy, Effective June 3, 2013. *TheMortgageReports.com*. Retrieved from http://themortgagereports.com/12740/new-fha-mortgage-insurance-premium-cancellation-policy-effective-june-3-2013

9. McCormally, K. (2011, January). What can 1 trillion buy. *Kiplinger.com*. Retrieved from http://www.kiplinger.com/slideshow/business/T019-S001-what-1-trillionwould-buy/index.html

10. Ellis, B. (2013, December 5). Average student loan debt: $29400. *CNNMoney.com*. Retrieved from http://money.cnn.com/2013/12/04/pf/college/student-loan-debt/

11. (2014). Loan Forgiveness. *Finaid.org*. Retrieved from http://www.finaid.org/loans/forgiveness.phtml

12. Rubin, R. and Collins, M. (2014, May 6). Early Tap of 401(k) Replaces Homes as American Piggy Bank. *Bloomberg.com*. Retrieved from http://www.bloomberg.com/news/2014-05-06/early-tap-of-401-k-replaces-homes-as-american-piggy-bank.html

13. Ramsey, D. (2013, September). The Total Money Makeover – A Proven Plan for Financial Fitness – Audiobook on CD.

14. (2014). Financial Statement. *Wikipedia.org*. Retrieved from http://en.wikipedia.org/wiki/Financial_statement

15. (2014). Earned Income. *IRS.gov*. Retrieved from http://www.irs.gov/Individuals/What-is-Earned-Income%3F

16. (2014). Passive Income. *Wikipedia.org*. Retrieved from http://en.wikipedia.org/wiki/Passive_income

17. (2014). Portfolio Income. *Investopedia.com*. Retrieved from http://www.investopedia.com/terms/p/portfolioincome.asp

18. (2014). Commodities. *Investopedia.com*. Retrieved from
http://www.investopedia.com/terms/c/commodity.asp

19. (2014). Certificate of Deposit. *Wikipedia.org*. Retrieved from
http://en.wikipedia.org/wiki/Certificate_of_deposit

20. (2014). 529 plan. *Wikipedia.org*. Retrieved from
http://en.wikipedia.org/wiki/529_plan

21. Copyright 2010 CSPN. All Rights Reserved. (2014). What is
a 529 Plan? *CollegeSavings.org*. Retrieved from
http://www.collegesavings.org/whatIs529.aspx

22. (2014). Montgomery GI Selected Reserve (MGIB-SR).
Benefits.VA.gov. Retrieved from
http://www.benefits.va.gov/gibill/mgib_sr.asp

23. (2014). Individual Retirement Account. *Wikipedia.org*.
Retrieved from
http://en.wikipedia.org/wiki/Individual_retirement_account

24. Copyright 2014 Cable News Network. A Time Warner
Company. All Rights Reserved. (2014). Annuities – What are the
disadvantages? *CNNMoney.com*. Retrieved from
http://money.cnn.com/retirement/guide/annuities_basics.moneym
ag/index.htm?iid=EL

25. (2014). LendingClub.com. Retrieved from
https://www.lendingclub.com/

26. (2014). Warren Buffet > Quotes > Quotable Quote.
Goodreads.com. Retrieved from

http://www.goodreads.com/quotes/29255-be-fearful-when-others-are-greedy-and-greedy-when-others

27. Fontinelle, A. (2014). Value Investing: Finding Undervalued Stocks. *Investopedia.com*. Retrieved from http://www.investopedia.com/university/value-investing/value-investing3.asp

28. Udland, M. (2014, August, 15). 30 Years Ago Warren Buffett Gave Away The Secret To Good Investing And Correctly Predicated No One Would Listen. *BusinessInsider.com*. Retrieved from http://www.businessinsider.com/warren-buffett-graham-and-doddsville-lecture-2014-8?utm_source=linkedin-bipage&utm_medium=referral

29. (2014). Watson (computer). *Wikipedia.org*. Retrieved from http://en.wikipedia.org/wiki/Watson_(computer)

30. (2014). Bond (finance) *Wikipedia.org*. Retrieved from http://en.wikipedia.org/wiki/Bond_(finance)

31. (2014). How to Invest in Bonds. *Wikihow.com*. Retrieved from http://www.wikihow.com/Invest-in-Bonds

32. Copyright 2014 Cable News Network. A Time Warner Company. All Rights Reserved. (2014). Basics of investing in mutual funds. *CNNMoney.com*. Retrieved from http://money.cnn.com/magazines/moneymag/money101/lesson6/

33. Fishman, S. (2014). Top Ten Tax Deductions for Landlords. *Nolo.com*. Retrieved from http://www.nolo.com/legal-encyclopedia/top-ten-tax-deductions-landlords-29497.html

34. Copyright 1997-2014 Intuit Inc. (2013). IRS Moving Expense Deductions. *TurboTax.com*. Retrieved from https://turbotax.intuit.com/tax-tools/tax-tips/General-Tax-Tips/IRS-Moving-Expense-Deductions/INF14389.html

35. Bell, K. (2013, February 22). Job hunting could help cut taxes. *Bankrate.com*. Retrieved from http://www.bankrate.com/finance/money-guides/deducting-job-search-costs.aspx

36. Copyright 1997-2014 Intuit Inc. (2013). Can I Write Off Credit Card Interest on My Taxes? *TurboTax.com*. Retrieved from https://turbotax.intuit.com/tax-tools/tax-tips/Tax-Deductions-and-Credits/Can-I-Write-Off-Credit-Card-Interest-on-My-Taxes--/INF14239.html

37. Hicken, M. (2013, August, 14). Average cost to raise a kid: $241,080. *CNNMoney.com*. Retrieved from http://money.cnn.com/2013/08/14/pf/cost-children/

38. Copyright 2014 Goodreads Inc. *Goodreads.com*. Retrieved from http://www.goodreads.com/quotes/92129-imagine-life-as-a-game-in-which-you-are-juggling

39. Sheridan, P. (2014, August, 14). I'm 57 and owe $152,000 in student loans. *CNNMoney.com*. Retrieved from http://money.cnn.com/2014/08/13/news/economy/older-student-debt/

40. Rawes, E. (2014, August, 08) 5 Worst Rates on Retailer Credit Cards. *WallStCheatSheet.com*. Retrieved from

http://wallstcheatsheet.com/personal-finance/5-worst-rates-on-retailer-credit-cards.html/?a=viewall

www.ingramcontent.com/pod-product-compliance
Lightning Source LLC
Chambersburg PA
CBHW021404170526
45164CB00002B/503